R. GUPTA'S®

SCIENCE

(PCM)

FORMULAE & DEFINITIONS

Ramesh Publishing House, New Delhi

Published by

O.P. Gupta *for* Ramesh Publishing House

Admin. Office

12-H, New Daryaganj Road, Opp. Officers' Mess

New Delhi-110002 ✆ 23275224, 23245124

E-mail: info@rameshpublishinghouse.com

For Online Shopping: www.rameshpublishinghouse.com

Showroom

- Balaji Market, Nai Sarak, Delhi-6 ✆ 23253720, 23282525
- 4457, Nai Sarak, Delhi-6, ✆ 23918938

Book Code: R-1010

26th Edition: June 2024

ISBN: 978-81-7812-526-8

Price: ₹ 60

Printed at: Deepak Offset, Delhi

CONTENTS

PHYSICS 7-116

CHEMISTRY 117-226

MATHS 227-336

PHYSICS

1

CURRENT ELECTRICITY

Electric Charge and Current

1. $I = \frac{\Delta Q}{\Delta t}$.

2. $I = ne$. **S.I. unit:** coul/sec = ampere.
   1 coul = 6.25×10^{18} electrons,
   1 amp = 6.25×10^{18} electrons/sec
   through a cross sectional area.

3. **Current density** $(\vec{J}) = \frac{I}{A}$.

   S.I. unit: amp.m^{-2}

   Where: A = cross sectional area $\perp^r$ to the direction of current, I.

4. V_d **(drift velocity of electrons)** $= \frac{I}{nAe} = \frac{\vec{J}}{ne}$.

   Where: n = number of free electrons volume.

5. Strength of storage cell ($A.H$) = charging current (amp) × time (hr). [1 amp × hr = 3600 coul].

Ohm's Law and Resistance

1. $I \propto V$ or $V = IR$ or $I = GV$, provided physical conditions (temperature, magnetic field, radiation etc) remain unchanged.

   Where: G = conductance $= \dfrac{1}{R}$

   [R = resistance]

   S.I. unit of G = mho = ohm^{-1}

   $$= \frac{1}{\text{ohm}} = \frac{\text{amp}}{\text{volt}} = \text{siemen}.$$

2. $R = \rho \dfrac{l}{A}$ **Where:** l = length of wire (along the direction of flow of I), A = cross sectional area ($\perp^r$ to the direction of flow of I) and ρ = specific resistance or electrical resistivity.

   σ = (electrical conductivity or specific conductance) $= \dfrac{1}{\rho}$.

S.I. unit of ρ and σ = ohm (Ω) × metre and mho/metre respectively.

3. $R = \rho \dfrac{l}{\pi r^2}$ $(A = \pi r^2$ for wire$) = \rho \dfrac{l}{\dfrac{\pi D^2}{4}}$.

Where: D = diameter.

4. $R = \dfrac{\rho V}{\pi^2 r^4}$ **Where:** V is the volume.

5. $R_t = R_0(1 + \alpha t)$

Where: α = temperature co-efficient of R.
Unit of α is per °C.

6. **To be remembered :**
   (*i*) 1 amp = 10^{-1} e.m.u. of $I = 3 \times 10^9$ e.s.u. of current.
   (*ii*) 1 coul = 10^{-1} e.m.u. of charge = 3×10^9 e.s.u. of charge.
   (*iii*) 1 volt = 10^8 e.m.u. of potential difference or 10^8 ab volt = $\dfrac{1}{300}$ e.s.u. of potential difference or $\dfrac{1}{300}$ stat volt.

(*iv*) 1 ohm (Ω) = 10^9 e.m.u. of $R = \frac{1}{9 \times 10^{11}}$ e.s.u. of R.

7. **Series grouping:** $R_s = r_1 + r_2 + r_3 + \ldots\ldots + r_n$.

8. **Parallel grouping:**

$$\frac{1}{R_p} = \frac{1}{r_1} + \frac{1}{r_2} + \frac{1}{r_3} + \ldots\ldots + \frac{1}{r_n}.$$

or $G = G_1 + G_2 + G_3 + \ldots\ldots + G_n$.

9. For two resistances in parallel :

$$R_p = \frac{r_1 r_2}{r_1 + r_2} = \frac{\text{product}}{\text{sum}}$$

10. For n identical resistances :

$R_s = nr$(series). $R_p = \frac{r}{n}$(parallel) and

$$\frac{R_s}{R_p} = n^2.$$

11. Approximate percentage change in $R = 2 \times$ small percentage change in length by stretching.

E.M.F., P.D. and Grouping of Cells

1. $\Delta V = \dfrac{\Delta W}{Q}$ or $\Delta W = Q\,\Delta V$.

   S.I. or practical unit of P.D. = Joule/coul = volt. **e.s.u.** of P.D. = erg/stat coul = stat volt. **e.m.u.** of P.D. = erg/ab coul = ab volt.

2. 1 ev = 1.6×10^{-19} Joule.
   1 Mev = 1.6×10^{-13} Joule (Mega ev).
   1 Bev = 1.6×10^{-10} Joule (Billion ev).

3. $I = \dfrac{E}{R+r}$ (closed circuit) or $E = V + Ir$.

   Where: E = e.m.f.,
   V = P.D., r = internal resistance, R = external resistance and Ir = potential drop.
   If, R = 0 (short circuit), I will be maximum,

   $$I_{max} = \frac{E}{r}.$$

   If, R = ∞ (open circuit), I will be minimum,

   $I_{min} = 0$.

4. **Series grouping of cells:**

   $$I = \frac{nE}{nr+R};\ I_{max} = \frac{E}{r}, \text{ when } R << r.$$

5. **Parallel grouping of cells:**

$$I = \frac{nE}{r + nR};\ I_{max} = \frac{nE}{r}\text{, when } r >> R.$$

6. **Mixed grouping of cells:**

$$I = \frac{mnE}{nr + mR};\ I_{max} = \frac{nE}{2R} = \frac{mE}{2r}\text{, when}$$

$nr = mR$.

Where: n = number of cells in one row,
m = number of rows and
$m \times n$ = total number of cells.

7. **Wrong series connection:**

$$I = \frac{(n - 2m)E}{R + nr};\quad I_{max} = \frac{(n - 2m)E}{nr}\text{, when}$$

$R << r$. **Where:** n = total number of cells and m = number of cells wrongly connected.

Wheatstone Bridge and Kirchoff's Law

1. When galvanometer shows no deflection, $PR = QS$
(i.e. products of alternate arms resistances are equal) or $\frac{P}{Q} = \frac{S}{R}$.

2. **1st law:** $\Sigma I = 0$ **2nd Law:** $\Sigma IR = \Sigma E$.
Where: E = total e.m.f. of the mesh or circuit.

Heating Effect of Current and Thermoelectricity

1. $Q = It$.
2. P.D. across ends of conductor, $V = IR$.
3. **Work done (*W*)** $= Q.V. = VIt = I^2Rt = \frac{V^2}{R} \times t$
   $= P \times t$.
4. **Power consumption (*P*)**
   $$= \frac{W}{t} = IV = I^2R = \frac{V^2}{R}.$$
5. **Heat produced (*H*)**
   $$= \frac{W}{J} = \frac{VIt}{J} = \frac{I^2Rt}{J} = \frac{V^2}{R} \times \frac{t}{J} = \frac{P}{J} \times t.$$
6. $P \times t =$ **Energy.**
7. **Practical unit** of energy supply = killo-watt-hour (kwh).
   1 I.B.O.T. unit = 1 kwh = 36×10^5 Joules.
8. **Number of units consumed**
   $$= \frac{\text{watt} \times \text{hr}}{1000} = \text{kwh}.$$
   S.I. unit: $I \to$ amp, $V \to$ volt, $R \to$ ohm, $t \to$ sec, $W \to$ Joule, $P \to$ watt, $J = 1$, $H \to$ Joule.

C.G.S. unit: 1 cal = 4.2 Joule, $H \rightarrow$ cal, $J = 4.2$ Joule/cal.

9. $H \propto R$, If I and t are constant, i.e.

$$\frac{H_1}{H_2} = \frac{R_1}{R_2}.$$

10. $H \propto \frac{1}{R}$ If V and t are constant, i.e.

$$\frac{H_1}{H_2} = \frac{R_2}{R_1}.$$

11. $H \propto I^2$. If R and t are constant.
12. $H \propto t$. If R and I are constant.
13. **Hot wire instrument** (for measuring both A.C. and D.C.) :

$$\theta \propto H \text{ or } \theta \propto t^2, \quad i.e. \frac{\theta_1}{\theta_2} = \frac{i_1^{\,2}}{i_2^{\,2}}.$$

14. $t_n = \frac{t_i + t_c}{2}$.

Where: t_n = neutral temperature
t_i = inversion temperature and
t_c = temperature of cold junction.

Chemical Effect of Current

1. **Charge** on one ion $= ne$.
   Where: n = valency of ion, e = electronic charge $= -1.6 \times 10^{-19}$ coul.

2. Number of ions liberated at electrode $= \frac{Q}{ne}$.
   Where: Q = charge flowing in electrolyte.

3. **Mass** of one atom $= \frac{A}{N}$.
   Where: A = atomic weight, N = Avogadro's number.

4. Mass of element (w) liberated at electrode = number of ions liberated × mass of one atom,
   i.e. $w = \frac{Q}{ne} \times \frac{A}{N} = \frac{1}{Ne} \times \frac{A}{n} \times Q = \frac{E}{F} \times Q.$
   Where: E = eq. wt.

5. $\frac{E}{F} = Z$ (electrochemical equivalent).
   S.I. unit of Z is kg/coul.

Shunt, Ammeter, Voltmeter and Branching of Current

1. To increase the range of an **ammeter** or to convert a **voltmeter** into an **ammeter**, a low

resistance (shunt) is connected in parallel.

$$S = \frac{G}{n-1} \text{ (in parallel)}. \ n = \frac{I}{I_g} = \frac{I_2}{I_1}.$$

Where: S = shunt resistance, G = resistance of ammeter, I_1 or I_g = current which the ammeter can measure and I_2 or I = current to be measured.

2. To increase the range of a **voltmeter** or to convert an **ammeter** into a **voltmeter**, a high resistance (R) is connected in series : $R = G(n-1)$.
   Where: G = resistance of voltmeter.

$$n = \frac{V}{V_g} \text{ or } \frac{V_2}{V_1} = \frac{\text{new range}}{\text{old range}}.$$

   Where: V_g or V_1 = voltage which the voltmeter can measure and V or V_2 = voltage to be measured.

3. Branching of current in two parallel resistances:

$$I_1 = \frac{Ir_2}{r_1 + r_2} \text{ and } I_2 = \frac{Ir_1}{r_1 + r_2}.$$

4. After shunting the decrease in resistance

$$= \frac{G^2}{G+S}.$$

Magnetic Effect of Current

Part–A: *Laplace's Law and Magnetic Field Induction*

1. **Laplace's law or Biot Savart law:**

$$\Delta B \text{(magnetic induction)} = \frac{\mu_0}{4\pi} \times \frac{i\Delta l \sin\theta}{r^2}.$$

Where: ΔB = magnetic induction (in weber/m^2 or tesla), Δl = very small length of conductor which carries a current i amp, r = radius vector making an angle θ with the direction of current (in meter), μ_0 = permeability of vacuum = $4\pi \times 10^{-7}$ henry/metre.

C.G.S. unit: $\Delta B \rightarrow$ gauss (1 weber/m^2 = 10^4 gauss).

2. Magnetic field induction due to current in a long straight wire:

$$B = \frac{\mu_0}{4\pi} \cdot \frac{2i}{r} = \frac{\mu_0 i}{2\pi r}.$$

3. Work done (W) in moving a unit pole around a long conductor:

$$W = \frac{\mu_0}{4\pi} \times 4\pi i = \mu_0 i .$$

4. (a) Magnetic field induction (B) due to current in a circular coil at its centre:

$$B = \frac{\mu_0}{4\pi} \times \frac{2\pi ni}{r} = \frac{\mu_0 ni}{2r} .$$

Where: n = number of turns of coil and

B always $\perp^r$ to the plane of coil.

(b) **At an axial pont:** $B = \dfrac{\mu_0}{4\pi} \times \dfrac{2\pi nir^2}{(r^2 + x^2)^{\frac{3}{2}}}$

Where: r = radius of coil, x = distance of the point on axis from centre of the coil.

5. Magnetic field induction (B) due to current in a **solenoid:**

(a) **B in central part:**

$$B = \frac{\mu_0}{4\pi} \times 4\pi ni = \mu_0 ni .$$

Where: n = number of turns per unit length.

(b) **B at ends:** $B' = \frac{\mu_0}{4\pi} \times 2\pi ni = \frac{\mu_0 ni}{2}$

N.B.: $B' = \frac{B}{2}$.

Part–B: ***Interaction of Magnetic Field and Electric Current***

1. Force on a current carrying conductor of length, l placed in a magnetic field of field induction B : $F = Bil \sin\theta$.
   Where: θ = angle made by conductor with magnetic field induction B in the direction of B.
   In S.I. system: $B \rightarrow$ weber/m^2, $i \rightarrow$ amp, $l \rightarrow$ meter, $F \rightarrow$ newton.
   In C.G.S., e.m.u.: $B \rightarrow$ gauss, $i \rightarrow$ e.m.u., $l \rightarrow$ cm, $F \rightarrow$ dyne.
2. (a) Force on a charged particle e, moving with velocity v entering magnetic field induction B at an angle θ:
   $$F = Bev \sin\theta$$
   Where: F in newton.

   (b) K.E. of particle $= \frac{P^2}{2m} = \frac{B^2e^2r^2}{2m}$.
   [momentum (P) = Ber].

Where

e = charge on particle,
m = mass of the particle and
r = radius described by the particle.

3. Force per unit length between two current carrying parallel conductors:

$$F = \frac{\mu_0}{4\pi} \times \frac{2i_1 i_2}{r} = \frac{\mu_0 i_1 i_2}{2\pi r} \text{ (S.I.).}$$

Part–C: Application in Galvanometer

1. **Tangent galvanometer:**

$$B = B_H \tan\theta (B \perp^r B_H) \text{ or } \frac{\mu_0 ni}{2r} = B_H \tan\theta$$

$$\text{or } i = \frac{2r\mathrm{B}_H}{\mu_0 n} \tan\theta = K \tan\theta, K = \frac{2rB_H}{\mu_0 n}.$$

Where: B = magnetic field induction, B_H = horizontal component of earth's field induction, θ = deflection of magnetic needle pivoted at the centre and K = reduction factor (same unit as current).

Unit of $B_H \rightarrow$ weber/m^2.

2. **Sine galvanometer : In S.I. system,**

$$B = B_H \sin\theta \text{ or } \frac{\mu_0 ni}{2r} = B_H \sin\theta$$

or $i = \frac{2rB_H}{\mu_0 n} \sin\theta = K\sin\theta.$

3. **Suspended coil galvanometer or moving coil galvanometer or D'Arsonval galvanometer :**

   (*i*) $F = Bil \sin\theta$, If $\theta = 0°$ or $180°$ then $F = 0$ and if $\theta = 90°$ then $F = Bil$.

   (*ii*) $i = \frac{C}{nAB}\theta = K\theta$ or $i \propto \theta$, i.e. $\frac{\theta_1}{\theta_2} = \frac{i_1}{i_2}$.

   Where: c = couple per unit twist, A = area of coil and n = number of turns.

Electromagnetic Induction

1. **Faraday's laws:**

   (*i*) The induced e.m.f. is directly proportional to the rate of change of flux, associated with circuit,

   i.e. $e \propto \frac{\Delta\phi}{\Delta t}$ or $e = K\frac{\Delta\phi}{\Delta t}$.

   In C.G.S., $e = n\frac{\Delta\phi}{\Delta t}$.

   Where: n = number of turns, $\Delta\phi \rightarrow$ maxwell, $e \rightarrow$ ab volt, $\Delta t \rightarrow$ sec.

   In S.I., $\Delta\phi \rightarrow$ weber, $e \rightarrow$ volt, $\Delta t \rightarrow$ sec.

   Relation: 1 weber = 10^8 maxwell.

(*ii*) Induced current $(I) = \frac{e}{R} = \frac{1}{R} \cdot \frac{\Delta\phi}{\Delta t}$.

(*iii*) Amount of charge that will flow

$$(q) = I \times \Delta t = \frac{\Delta\phi}{R}.$$

2. Combined form of both **Faraday's and Lenz's law:**

$$e = -\frac{\Delta\phi}{\Delta t} \text{ (one turn)}, \quad e = -n\frac{\Delta\phi}{\Delta t} \text{ (}n\text{ turns)}.$$

3. **Self Induction:** $e_1 = -L\frac{\Delta i}{\Delta t}$.

Where: $\frac{\Delta i}{\Delta t}$ = rate of change of current,

e_1 = induced e.m.f. and L = co-efficient of self inductance.

S.I. unit of L is ohm × sec = henry = 10^9 e.m.u (ab henry).

4. **Mutual Inductance :** $e_2 = -M\frac{\Delta i}{\Delta t}$.

Where: M is mutual inductance,

S.I. unit → henry.

Transformer

1. **For an ideal transformer :**

$$V \propto N \text{ or } I \propto \frac{1}{N} \text{ or } \frac{V_2}{V_1} = \frac{I_1}{I_2} = \frac{N_2}{N_1}$$

or $I_1 V_1$ (input power) $= I_2 V_2$ (output power), **Where:** N_2 and N_1 = number of turns in secondary and primary coils, V_2 (output) and V_1 (input) are voltage across secondary and primary and I_2 (output) and I_1 (input) are currents across secondary and primary.

2. $\frac{N_2}{N_1}$ = **Transformation ratio** $= K$.

3. **Efficiency** $= \frac{\text{output wattage}}{\text{input wattage}}$

4. **Percentage efficiency**

$$= \frac{\text{output wattage}}{\text{input wattage}} \times 100$$

Alternating (Sinusoidal) Current

1. $\phi = nAB \cos \omega t$. **Where:** ωt = angle between direction of B and normal to coil.
   Induced e.m.f. $(e) = nAB\omega \sin \omega t = e_0 \sin \omega t$.

Where: n = number of turns of the coil, A = area of the coil, B = magnetic field induction, ω (angular velocity of coil) = $2\pi f$ and f (frequency) = number of revolutions/sec. **In S.I. :** $A \rightarrow$ m^2, $B \rightarrow$ weber/m^2, $\omega \rightarrow$ rad/sec and $e \rightarrow$ volt.

2. $e = e_0 \sin \omega t$ and $I = I_0 \sin \omega t$. They are called sinusoidal or periodic or alternating voltage and current.

Where:

e and I = instantaneous voltage and current,

e_0 and I_0 = maximum or peak voltage and current,

ωt = phase angle,

ω = angular velocity or angular frequency and

$\frac{\omega}{2\pi}$ = frequency (f) = $\frac{1}{T}$.

3. **Average voltage and current:** average value over half cycle = $\frac{2}{\pi} \times$ maximum or peak value. Hence, $I_{av} = \frac{2}{\pi} \times I_0$ and $e_{av} = \frac{2}{\pi} \times e_0$.

4. **R.M.S. or virtual or effective value**

$$= \frac{\text{peak value}}{\sqrt{2}}, \text{ i.e. } I_{r.m.s} = \frac{I_0}{\sqrt{2}} \text{ and}$$

$$e_{r.m.s} = \frac{e_0}{\sqrt{2}}.$$

5. **Form factor** $= \dfrac{\text{R.M.S. value}}{\text{average value}} \simeq 1.1$ and is constant.

6. **Phase relations in A.C. circuits:**

(*i*) In case of circuit containing only resistance : $i = \dfrac{E}{R}$.

Where: E = e.m.f and R = resistance.

(*ii*) Circuit with resistance and inductance (L):

$$i = \frac{E}{\sqrt{R^2 + (L\omega)^2}} = \frac{E}{Z}$$

Where: Z is called impedance and is the effective resistance of an A.C. circuit and $L\omega$ is called inductive reactance.

(*iii*) Circuit with R and C: $i = \dfrac{E}{\sqrt{R^2 + \left(\dfrac{1}{C\omega}\right)^2}}$.

Where: $\frac{1}{C\omega}$ = capacitive reactance and

impedance $(Z) = \sqrt{R^2 + \left(\frac{1}{C\omega}\right)^2}$

(*iv*) Circuit with *R*, *L* and *C* :

$$i = \frac{E}{\sqrt{R^2 + \left(L\omega - \frac{1}{C\omega}\right)^2}}.$$

$$\text{Reactance} = L\omega - \frac{1}{C\omega}.$$

$$Z = \sqrt{R^2 + \left(L\omega - \frac{1}{C\omega}\right)^2}$$

Condition for resonance:

frequency $(f) = \frac{1}{2\pi} \cdot \sqrt{\frac{1}{LC}}$

In this case :

$$i = \frac{E}{R}, \text{ since } \left(L\omega - \frac{1}{C\omega}\right)^2 = 0.$$

2

MODERN PHYSICS

Photoelectric Effect

1. **Symbols used:** N = number of photoelectrons emitted, I = intensity of light, E_K = kinetic energy of photoelectrons, P = illuminating power, d = distance from photocell, ϕ = work function for the photometal, υ = frequency of incident radiation, υ_0 = threshold frequency, λ = wavelength of incident radiation, λ_0 = threshold wavelength, v = velocity, h = planck's constant, m = mass of the electron, e = electronic charge = -1.6×10^{-19} coul, V_s = stopping potential and V_{max} = maximum velocity of the electron.
2. **Laws of photoelectric effect:**

   (a) **1st law:** $N \propto I$, N is independent of υ of the incident radiation or $N \propto \dfrac{P}{d^2}$.

(b) **2nd law:** V or $E_K \propto \upsilon$ but independent of I.

3. **For a given photometal:** $\phi = h\upsilon_0 = \dfrac{hc}{\lambda_0}$

Unit of ϕ = electron volt,

$h = 6.62 \times 10^{-34}$ Joule.sec.

4. $V_{max} = \sqrt{\dfrac{2eV_s}{m}}$ or $\dfrac{1}{2}mv^2{}_{max} = eV_s$.

5. **Einstein's photoelectric equation:**

$$\frac{1}{2}mv^2{}_{max} = h(\upsilon - \upsilon_0) = \frac{hc}{\lambda} - \frac{hc}{\lambda_0}$$

$$h\upsilon = h\upsilon_0 + \frac{1}{2}mv_{max}^2 = \phi + \frac{1}{2}mv_{max}^2.$$

Thermionic Valves (Diode and Triode)

1. **Amplification factor,** $\mu = \dfrac{\Delta V_p}{\Delta V_g}$,

I_p = constant. [$\mu > 1$ always].

2. **Dynamic plate resistance,**

$$R_p = \frac{\Delta V_p}{\Delta I_p}, V_g = \text{constant}.$$

3. **Mutual or transconductance,**

$$G_m = \frac{\Delta I_p}{\Delta V_g},\ V_p = \text{constant.}$$

S.I. unit of $G_m = \text{ohm}^{-1}$, mho or siemen.

4. $\mu = R_p \times G_m$.

5. **Gain in voltage,** $m = \dfrac{\mu R_l}{R_p + R_l}$.

Where: R_l = load resistance.

Radioactivity

1. $T_a = \dfrac{1}{\lambda}$ **Where:** T_a = mean life or average life, λ = disintegration constant.

2. **Half life,** $T_{\frac{1}{2}} = 0.693 \times T_a = 69.3\%$ of T_a

or $T_{\frac{1}{2}} = \dfrac{0.693}{\lambda} = \dfrac{\log e^2}{\lambda}$

3. $\dfrac{N}{N_o} = \left(\dfrac{1}{2}\right)^n$ **Where:** N_o = original amount or number of nuclei, N = number of

undisintegrated nuclei after time t,

n = number of half lives passed and $n = \frac{t}{T}$.

4. **Percentage radioactivity** $= \left(\frac{1}{2}\right)^n \times 100$.

Atomic Structure

1. $r_n = \frac{\epsilon_0 n^2 h^2}{\pi m Z e^2}$. For the 1st orbit, $n = 1$

$\therefore r_1 = \frac{\epsilon_0 h^2}{\pi m Z e^2}$ or $r_n = n^2 r_1$

Where: r_n = radius of nth orbit.

2. $V_n = \frac{Ze^2}{2 \epsilon_0 nh}$ or $V_n = \frac{V_1}{n}$

(for hydrogen atom $Z = 1$).

Where: V_n = velocity of electron in n^{th} orbit and V_1 = velocity in 1st orbit.

3. $E_n = -\frac{mZ^2 e^4}{8 \epsilon_0^2 n^2 h^2}$.

For $n = 1$,

$$E_1 = -\frac{mZ^2e^4}{8\epsilon_0^2 h^2} \text{ or } E_n = -\frac{E_1}{n^2}.$$

Where: E_n and E_1 are energy of electron in n^{th} and 1st orbit respectively.

4. $I\omega_n = mv_nr_n = \dfrac{nh}{2\pi}$.

Discharge Phenomena and Cathode Rays

1. **Paschen's law:** $V \propto P.\, d$ (for a particular discharge tube).
   Where: V = ionising potential, P = pressure inside the tube and d = separation between electrodes.
2. Force (F) on a charged particle in a magnetic field:
   $F = Bev \sin\theta$ ($F \perp^r$ to B and $F \perp^r$ to v also);

   or $\vec{F} = e(\vec{B} \times \vec{v})$.

   Where: θ = angle between B and v and v = velocity of particle.
3. Radius (r) of circle described by charged particle:

$$Bev = \frac{mv^2}{r} \text{ (taking } \theta = 90°) \text{ or } r = \frac{mv}{Be} = \frac{P}{Be}$$

4. **Effect of electric field:** $\vec{F} = e.\vec{E} (\vec{F} \| \vec{E})$. **Where:** e = charge of the particle, E = electric field.

N.B. If $\vec{V} \perp^r \vec{E}$, path will be parabolic.

Electromagnetic Wave and X-Ray

1. $C_m = \frac{1}{\sqrt{\mu \in}}$. For air or vacuum $C_0 = \frac{1}{\sqrt{\mu_0 \in_0}}$.
   Where: C_m and C_0 are velocity of e.m.t. wave in medium and vaccum.
2. **Energy of single quanta or photon** ***(E)*** $= hv$.
3. **Properties of photon :** (*i*) **rest mass** $= 0$.
   (*ii*) **charge** $= 0$. (*iii*) **energy** $= E = hv = \frac{hc}{\lambda}$.
   (*iv*) **momentum** ***(P)*** $= mc = \frac{hv}{c} = \frac{h}{\lambda}$.
   (*v*) **moving mass** $= \frac{hv}{c^2} = \frac{h}{\lambda c}$.
   (*vi*) $C_0 = 3 \times 10^8$ m/s. (*vii*) **spin** $= 1$.

4. Intensity of X-ray $\propto$ filament temperature **(collidge tube).**

5. $E = eV = \frac{1}{2}mv^2 = h\upsilon_{max} = \frac{hc}{\lambda_{min}}$

   or $\upsilon_{max} = \frac{eV}{h}$ & $\lambda_{min} = \frac{hc}{eV}$.

   Where: V= applied accelerating potential to the tube, v = speed of incident electron and E= energy.

6. **Moseley's law:** $\upsilon \propto Z^2$ (Z = atomic number of the element).

7. Absorption of X-ray $\propto Z$.

   Absorption of X-ray $\propto \frac{1}{\lambda}$

8. $K \propto Z^2$ **Where:** K= absorption co-efficient

9. **Rontgen is the unit of X-ray dose.**

   1 Curie = 3.7×10^{10} disintegrations/sec
   1 Rutherford = 10^6 disintegrations/sec

Nuclear Energy, Mass Defect and Binding Energy

1. $E = mc^2$
2. $1ev = 1.6 \times 10^{-19}$ Joule $= 1.6 \times 10^{-12}$ erg.

3. 1 a.m.u. = 1.66×10^{-27} kg = 1.66×10^{-24} gm $\simeq$ 931 Mev.

4. $\Delta m = [ZM_p + (A - Z)M_n] - M.$

   Where: Δm = mass defect, Z = atomic number, A = mass number, M = mass of nucleus, M_p = mass of proton and M_n = mass of neutron.

5. **Binding energy** = $\Delta m \times C^2$.

6. **Packing fraction** = $\dfrac{\Delta m}{A} \times 10^4$.

3

GENERAL PHYSICS

Units

1. $N_1U_1 = N_2U_2$.
2. **Fundamental or basic S.I. units:**

   (*i*) **metre** (m) → length. (*ii*) **kg** → mass. (*iii*) **second** (s) → time. (*iv*) **kelvin** (K) → temperature. (*v*) **ampere** (A) → electric current. (*vi*) **candela** (Cd) → luminous intensity. (*vii*) **mole** (mol) → amount of substance.
3. **Supplementary S.I. units :**

   (*i*) plane angle : radian (rad).

   (*ii*) solid angle : steradian (Sr).
4. **Prefixes used for multiples and sub-multiples:**

10^1 = deca (D)	10^2 = hecto (H)	10^3 = kilo (K)	10^6 = mega (M)
10^9 = giga (G)	10^{12} = tera (T)	10^{15} = peta (P)	10^{18} = exa (E)

Sub-Multiples

10^{-1} = deci (d)	10^{-2} = centi (c)	10^{-3} = milli (m)	10^{-6} = micro (μ)
10^{-9} = nano (n)	10^{-12} = pico (p)	10^{-15} = femto (f)	10^{-18} = atto (at)

5. **Some other Important units:**

(*i*) 1 micron (μ) = 10^{-6} m.

(*ii*) 1 millimicron (mμ) = 10^{-9} m.

(*iii*) 1 angstrom unit (A.U.) = 10^{-10} m.

(*iv*) 1 X-ray unit (X.U.) = 10^{-13} m.

(*v*) 1 fermi = 10^{-15} m (used in nuclear physics).

(*vi*) 1 light year = 10^{16} m (approximately).

(*vii*) 1 par second = 3.26 light years.

(*viii*) 1 sea mile = 6020 ft.

(*ix*) 1 cable = 182.5 m.

(*x*) 1 knot = 1 sea mile/hr or 1 nautical mile/hr.

(*xi*) 1 slug = 14.59 kg.

(*xii*) 1 bar = 10^5 N/m^2.

6. To change one system of units into another :

$$N_2 = N_1\left(\frac{M_1}{M_2}\right)^x \cdot \left(\frac{L_1}{L_2}\right)^y \cdot \left(\frac{T_1}{T_2}\right)^z.$$

Where: N_1 = numerical value in one system and N_2 = numerical value in another system.

Vectors and Scalars, Velocity and Acceleration

1. (*i*) $\vec{V} \times S = \vec{V}$. (*ii*) $\frac{\vec{V}}{S} = \vec{V}$. (*iii*) $\vec{V} . \vec{V} = S$.

   (*iv*) $\vec{V} \times \vec{V} = \vec{V}$.

2. $\vec{A} = K \vec{a}$.

3. $\vec{A} = Ax^{\hat{e}} + Ay^{\hat{j}} + Az^{\hat{k}}$, also

   $|A| = \sqrt{A_x^2 + A_y^2 + A_z^2}$.

4. **Dot or Scalar product:**

   $\vec{A} . \vec{B} = |A| . |B| \cos\theta$.

   Where: θ is angle between $\vec{A}$ and $\vec{B}$ measured from A to B.

5. **Vector or cross product:**

   $\vec{C} = \vec{A} \times \vec{B} = |A| . |B| \sin\theta_n$.

6. **Instantaneous velocity:** $(v_i) = \frac{dy}{dt}$.

7. **Average velocity** $(\vec{V_a})$

$$= \frac{\text{total displacement}}{\text{total time taken}} = \frac{y_2 - y_1}{t_2 - t_1} = \frac{\Delta \vec{y}}{\Delta t}.$$

8. **Average speed** $= \dfrac{\text{total distance travelled}}{\text{total time taken}}$

9. **Change in velocity** $(\Delta \vec{V})$

$= \text{final velocity } (\vec{V}_2) - \text{initial velocity } (\vec{V}_1)$.

10. **Average acceleration** $(\vec{f_a})$

$$= \frac{\text{change in velocity}}{\text{time interval}} = \frac{\Delta \vec{V}}{\Delta t}.$$

11. **Instantaneous acceleration** $(f_i) = \dfrac{dv}{dt}$.

12. Relative velocity of A with respect to

$B(\vec{V}_{AB}) = \vec{V}_A - \vec{V}_B$.

13. **Composition and resolution of velocities and forces:**

$$R^2 = v_1^2 + v_2^2 + 2v_1v_2\cos\theta,$$

and $\tan\alpha = \dfrac{v_2\sin\theta}{v_1 + v_2\cos\theta}$.

$R_{max} = v_1 + v_2$, when $\theta = 0°$;

$R_{min} = v_1 - v_2$, when $\theta = 180°$.

$$v_1 = \frac{R\sin\beta}{\sin(\alpha+\beta)},\ v_2 = \frac{R\sin\alpha}{\sin(\alpha+\beta)}.$$

Where: $\theta = \alpha + \beta$.

Components at right angle: $v_1 = R\cos\alpha$ and $v_2 = R\sin\alpha$.

N.B.: For forces, replace v_1 by P and v_2 by Q.

Equation of Motion Along a Line

1. **In horizontal plane, with uniform velocity and acceleration:**
   (*i*) $s = ut$, $[f = 0]$. (*ii*) $v = u + ft$. (*iii*) $v^2 = u^2 + 2fs$.
   (*iv*) $s = ut + \frac{1}{2}ft^2$. (*v*) The distance travelled in n^{th} second, $S_n = u + \frac{1}{2}(2n-1)f$.

N.B.: For rotational motion, replace u, v, s and f by ω_0, ω, θ and α respectively.

2. **For motion under gravity:** (*i*) $g = 9.8\text{ m/sec}^2$ (*ii*) $s = h$ (*iii*) $f = \pm g$ for downward and upward motion respectively. (*iv*) $h_{max} = \frac{u^2}{2g}$ (for upward). (*v*) $\frac{2u}{g}$ = total time of flight = time to ascend + time to descend.
3. For motion on an inclined plane making an angle α with the horizontal plane, replace g by $\pm g \sin\alpha$, for downward and upward motion respectively.

Projectile Motion

When: angle of projection = θ.

1. **Time of flight (T)** $= \frac{2v\sin\theta}{g}$.
2. **Maximum vertical height (H)**

$$= \frac{v^2\sin^2\theta}{2g};\ H_{max} = \frac{V^2}{2g}, \text{ when } \theta = 90°.$$

3. **Horizontal range (*R*)** $= \dfrac{v^2 \sin 2\theta}{g}$;

$R_{max} = \dfrac{v^2}{g}$, when $\theta = 45°$.

4. Range for θ = Range for $(90° - \theta)$ for the same velocity.

5. At maximum height K.E. $= \dfrac{1}{2}mv^2 \cos^2\theta$

   and at lowest point, K.E. $= \dfrac{1}{2}mv^2$, hence their ratio $= \cos^2\theta$.

6. Horizontal projection from height (h); time to reach the ground $(t) = \sqrt{\dfrac{2h}{g}}$.

Newton's Laws of Motion

1. **Momentum (*P*)** $= mv$.

2. **Force (*F*)** $= \dfrac{dp}{dt} = mf$.

N.B. : For rotational motion replace, m, F and P by I, τ and L respectively.

3. **Impulse** = $F.t = P_2 - P_1$ = change in momentum.
4. **Units of Force:** Absolute → 1 Newton (S.I.) = 10^5 dyne **(c.g.s)**,

   1 gravitational unit = $g \times$ absolute unit.
5. $R = m(g \pm f)$ are reactions of mass m, moving on a lift upward and downward respectively.
6. **Time period of a pendulum inside a moving lift:**

   gT^2 (normal) = $(g + f)\ T_1^2$ (ascending) = $(g - f)\ T_2^2$ (descending).

   $\frac{g}{n^2}$ (normal) = $\frac{g+f}{n_1^2}$ (ascending) = $\frac{g-f}{n_2^2}$ (descending).

Work, Energy and Power

1. **Work (W)** = $\vec{F}.\vec{x}\cos\theta$.

   When $\theta = 90°$, $W = 0$ and when $\theta = 180°$, W is –ve.

2. **Power** $(\vec{P}) = \frac{W}{t} = \vec{F}.\vec{v} = F.\,v\cos\theta$

$= \text{force} \times \text{velocity}.$

3. **Kinetic Energy (K.E.)**

$= \frac{1}{2}mv^2 = \frac{P^2}{2m}$

$= \frac{1}{2}Pv = \frac{mv^2}{2g}$ (gravitational K.E.)

4. **Work done by the resultant force**

$(W) = F \times x = \frac{1}{2}m({v_2}^2 - {v_1}^2).$

5. **Stopping distance** $(d) = \frac{\frac{1}{2}mv^2}{F}$

$= \frac{\text{initial K.E.}}{\text{retarding force}}$

6. In a frictionless gravitational field :

$\text{K.E.}(\frac{1}{2}mv^2) + P.E.(mgh) = \text{constant}.$

7. K.E. never be –ve but P.E. may be –ve or + ve.

8. **Work done by a variable force (W)** $= \int F.dx.$

9. **Spring force (F)** $= \pm Kx$. **Where:** K = spring constant and $\pm x$ = stretched or compressed distance respectively.

10. P.E. stored in a spring compressed through the distance $x = \frac{1}{2} Kx^2$.

11. **Units of work:** Absolute, 1 Joule **(S.I.)** = 10^7 erg **(c.g.s).**

    Gravitational **S.I.** → kg.m., **c.g.s** → gm. cm.

    In nuclear physics → Electron volt (ev).

12. **Units of power and relation:** Absolute, **S.I. :** Joul/sec = watt, **c.g.s:** erg/sec. **Special unit: Horse Power (H.P.)** = 550 ft. lb/sec = 746 watt.

Conservation of Linear Momentum and Collision

1. $\Sigma \vec{P}$ = constant, when external force = 0.
2. Total momentum before collision = total momentum after collision, i.e.

$$P_1 + P_2 = P_1' + P_2'.$$

3. **For perfect elastic collision:**

$$m_1u_1 + m_2u_2 = m_1v_1 + m_2v_2 \text{ and}$$

$$\frac{1}{2}m_1{u_1}^2 + \frac{1}{2}m_2{u_2}^2 = \frac{1}{2}m_1{v_1}^2 + \frac{1}{2}m_2{v_2}^2.$$

$[r = 1]$.

4. **Co-efficient of restitution (r)**

$$= \frac{\text{relative velocity after collision}}{\text{relative velocity before collision}}$$

$= \dfrac{v_2 - v_1}{u_1 - u_2}$, when $u_1 > u_2$. $r = \sqrt{\dfrac{h}{H}}$.

Where: h = rebounding height

H = falling height.

Parallel Forces, Moment, Couple and Friction

1. $R = P \pm Q$, for like and (unlike unequal, $P > Q$) || forces respectively.
2. If P, Q and R act at points A, B, C respectively || to each other and A B C is a straight line then $\dfrac{P}{BC} = \dfrac{Q}{AC} = \dfrac{R}{AB}$.

3. **Moment of a couple (*M*)** = F.x = force × arm of the couple.

4. **Moment of a force** $(\vec{M}) = \vec{F}.\vec{r}$

5. **Frictional force (*F*)** = μR.
   Where: μ = co-efficient of friction.

6. **For same surfaces:** $\mu_s > \mu_k > \mu_r$.

   Where: μ_s, μ_k and μ_r are co-efficients of limiting or static, kinetic and rolling friction respectively.

7. $\mu = \tan\lambda$. **Where:** λ = angle of friction.
8. $\mu = \tan\theta$. **Where:** θ = angle of repose.
9. **Minimum force required to just slide a body over a rough horizontal surface**

   (F) = $\mu_s mg$.

10. $F = \mu_k mg$, for maintaining a body to slide with uniform speed over a rough horizontal surface.
11. **Motion on a rough inclined plane:**
    (*i*) Minimum force required to prevent the body from sliding down (*F*)
    $= mg(\sin\theta - \mu_s \cos\theta)$

(*ii*) Minimum force required to slide a body up the plane :
$F = mg(\sin\theta + \mu_k \cos\theta)$.
Where: θ = angle of inclination.

Uniform Circular Motion

1. $v = r\omega$.
2. **Radial or centripetal acceleration (f_r)**
$$= \frac{v^2}{r} = r\omega^2 = v\omega.$$
3. **Tangential acceleration (f_t)**
$$= \frac{dv}{dt} = r\frac{d\omega}{dt} = r\alpha.$$
Where: α = angular acceleration.
4. **Instantaneous acceleration (f)**
$$= \sqrt{f_r^2 + f_t^2}.$$
5. **Centripetal force** $= \frac{mv^2}{r} = mr\omega^2 = mv\omega =$ **centrifugal reaction** in opposite direction.
6. **Motion of a cyclist :** $\tan\theta = \frac{v^2}{rg}$.
Where: θ = angle of inclination from vertical.

7. **Banking of track:** $\tan\theta = \frac{v^2}{rg}$.

Where: θ = angle of banking.

8. **Maximum speed for safe driving :**

$v = \sqrt{\mu rg}$.

9. **Motion in a vertical circle:**

(*i*) Tension at the top (T_1)

$= \frac{mv_1^2}{r} - mg$.

(*ii*) Tension at the bottom (T_2)

$= \frac{mv_2^2}{r} + mg$.

(*iii*) $T_2 - T_1 = 6\,mg$.

(*iv*) $v_2^2 - v_1^2 = 4rg$.

(*v*) Minimum speed at the top to maintain the body moving $(v_1) = \sqrt{rg}$.

(*vi*) Minimum speed at the bottom to maintain the body moving $(v_2) = \sqrt{5rg}$.

Surface Tension

1. **Surface tension (T)** $= \dfrac{F}{l}$.

   S.I. unit $\rightarrow \mathrm{N} \times m^{-1}$.

2. **Surface energy (S)** $= \dfrac{W}{A}$.

   S.I. unit $\rightarrow$ Joule $\times m^{-2}$.

3. Excess pressure (P) inside a liquid drop

   $= \dfrac{2T}{r}$. **Where:** r = radius.

4. Excess pressure (P) inside a soap bubble

   $= \dfrac{4T}{r}$.

5. Work done (W) in blowing a soap bubble $= 8\pi r^2 \times S$.

6. (*i*) $T = \dfrac{rhpg}{2\cos\theta}$. For pure water ($\theta = 0°$),

   $T = \dfrac{1}{2} rhpg$.

(*ii*) If the effective height $(h) = \frac{1}{3}r$, then

$$T = \frac{r(h + \frac{1}{3}r)\rho g}{2\cos\theta}.$$

Where: θ = angle of contact, h = rise of liquid, r = radius of the capillary tube and ρ = density of the liquid.

7. **Jurin's law :** $h \propto \frac{1}{r}$. If ρ, g, θ and T are constant, i.e. hr = constant.

Fluids in Motion and Viscosity

1. **Rate of flow (*R*)** $= A \times v$.
   Where: A = cross-sectional area and
   v = velocity of flow.
2. **Equation of continuity:** For stream line flow and incompressible fluid, Av = constant, i.e. $A_1v_1 = A_2v_2$.
3. **Bernoulli's theorem:**
   (*i*) Pressure energy, P.E. and K.E. per unit volume are constant,

   i.e. $P + \rho gh + \frac{1}{2}\rho v^2 = \text{constant}.$

(*ii*) If $\frac{\text{energy}}{\text{mass}}$ is considered:

$$\frac{P}{\rho} + gh + \frac{1}{2}v^2 = \text{constant.}$$

Where: h = height, ρ = density and P = pressure at any point.

(*iii*) $\frac{P}{\rho} + \frac{1}{2}v^2 = \text{constant.}$ ($\because$ P.E. = 0) in a horizontal plane.

4. **Torricelli's theorem:**

(*i*) $v = \sqrt{2gh}$. (*ii*) $t = \sqrt{\frac{2h_1}{g}}$.

(*iii*) $x = 2\sqrt{hh_1}$.

Where: h = height of the liquid layer above the orfice, h_1 = height of the orfice above the ground, x = range, v = velocity of efflux and t = time to fall to the ground.

5. $F = -\eta A \frac{dv}{dx}$.

6. **Poiseculle's equation :** $V = \frac{\pi P r^4}{8\eta l}$.

7. **Stoke's law :** $F = 6\pi\eta r v$.

8. $v_t = \frac{2}{9}.\frac{r^2(\rho - \sigma)g}{\eta}$. **Where:** v_t = terminal velocity, ρ and σ = density of the material and fluid.

9. $v_c = \frac{K\eta}{\rho r}$. **Where:** ρ = density of liquid, r = radius of the tube and K = **Renold's number.**

Elasticity

1. **Stress** = $\frac{F}{A}$; **S.I. unit** → N.m^{-2}

2. **Strain** = $\frac{\text{change in some measure}}{\text{total measure}}$

3. **Stress** = $E \times$ strain **(Hooke's law).** **Where:** E = Elastic constant or modulus of elasticity.

4. $\gamma = \frac{\text{tensile stress}}{\text{tensile strain}} = \frac{\frac{F}{A}}{\frac{l}{L}}$ (for solids only).

   Where: l = change in length, L = original length. γ = **Young's modulus** of elasticity.

5. **K (Bulk modulus)** $= \dfrac{\text{volume stress}}{\text{volume strain}}$, (for solids, liquids and gases) $= \dfrac{\frac{F}{A}}{\frac{v}{V}}$.

Where: v = change in volume, V = original volume.

S.I. unit $\rightarrow$ N.m^{-2}

6. **Shearing or rigidity modulus (η)**

$$= \frac{\text{shearing stress}}{\text{shearing strain}} = \frac{F}{A.\theta}$$

Where: θ = shearing angle,

S.I. unit $\rightarrow$ N.m^{-2}.

7. **Two types of Bulk modulus (K):**

   (*i*) **Isothermal** $K = P$ (P = pressure of the gas).

   (*ii*) **Adiabatic** $K = \gamma P$, $\gamma = \dfrac{C_p}{C_v}$.

8. **Relation between, γ, K and η :**

$$\frac{9}{\gamma} = \frac{3}{\eta} = \frac{1}{K}.$$

9. **Poisson's ratio** $(\sigma) = \dfrac{\text{lateral strain}}{\text{longitudinal strain}}$

$$= \frac{\frac{d}{D}}{\frac{l}{L}} = \frac{dL}{lD}.$$ **Where:** d = change in diameter, D = original diameter.

10. Work done (W) in stretching a spring or P.E. of a stretched spring : $W = \frac{1}{2}Kx^2$.

    Where: $K = \dfrac{F}{x}$ = spring constant.

11. **Compressibility** $= \dfrac{1}{K}$.

12. **Safety factor** $= \dfrac{\text{breaking stress}}{\text{working stress}}$.

13. Work done (W) in stretching a wire or the energy stored in stretched wire:

    $W = \frac{1}{2} \times \text{stress} \times \text{strain} \times \text{volume}.$

Simple Harmonic Motion and Pendulum

1. **For S.H.M:** $f \propto -y$. **Where:** f = acceleration, y = displacement.
2. (*i*) $y = a \sin(\omega t + \phi)$.

   Where: $\omega = \frac{2\pi}{T} = 2\pi n =$ angular frequency, a=amplitude, $\omega t + \phi$ =phase and ϕ = epoch or initial phase.

   (*ii*) At mean position, $y = 0$.

   In this case : $y = a \sin \omega t$.
3. (*i*) $v = a\omega \cos(\omega t + \phi) = \omega\sqrt{a^2 - y^2}$.

   (*ii*) $v_{max} = a\omega$, at $y = 0$, i.e. at the mean position.

   (*iii*) $v_{min} = 0$, at $y = \pm a$, i.e. at the turning points.
4. (*i*) $f = -a\omega^2 \sin(\omega t + \phi) = -\omega^2 y$.

   (*ii*) $f_{max} = \pm\omega^2 a$, at $y = \pm a$.

   (*iii*) $f_{min} = 0$, at $y = 0$.

5. (*i*) $\text{K.E.} = \frac{1}{2} m \omega^2 (a^2 - y^2)$.

(*ii*) $\text{P.E.} = \frac{1}{2} m \omega^2 y^2$.

(*iii*) Total energy = K.E. + P.E. = $\frac{1}{2} m \omega^2 a^2$

(always constant).

6. Time period of oscillating spring:

$$T = 2\pi \sqrt{\frac{m}{K}}.$$

7. Simple pendulum : $T = 2\pi \sqrt{\frac{l}{g}}$.

8. Compound pendulum:

$$T = 2\pi \sqrt{\frac{L}{g}}.$$

Where: $L = l + \frac{K^2}{l}$, l = distance of C.G. from the support, K = radius of gyration about an axis passing through C.G. and || to the axis of oscillation.

9. **Torsional pendulum:**

$$T = 2\pi\sqrt{\frac{l}{C}}\,.$$

Rotation and Moment of Inertia

1. **K.E. of a rolling body** $= \frac{1}{2}mv^2 + \frac{1}{2}I\omega^2$

2. **M.I. (I)** $= m_1r_1{}^2 + m_2r_2{}^2 + \ldots\ldots\ldots$

$$= \Sigma mr^2 = MK^2\,.$$

3. **Theorem of parallel axis :** $I = I_{c.g.} + Mx^2$.

4. **Theorem of $\perp^r$ axis:** $I_z = I_x + I_y$, [$\perp^r$ to each other].

5. **M.I. of a thin uniform rod of length l and mass M:**

   (a) Axis through its centre and $\perp^r$ to length :

$$I = \frac{Ml^2}{12}$$

   (b) Through one end and $\perp^r$ to length:

$$I = \frac{1}{3}Ml^2$$

6. **M.I. of a rectangular lamina :**

(a) Axis through its centre and $\perp^r$ to the plane :

$$I = \frac{M}{12}(l^2 + b^2).$$

(b) Through centre and || to length or breadth : $I = \frac{Ml^2}{12}$ or $\frac{Mb^2}{12}$.

7. M.I. of a **circular ring** or **loop** about an axis:

(a) Through centre and $\perp^r$ to the plane : $I = Mr^2$.

(b) Through a diameter : $I = \frac{1}{2}Mr^2$.

8. M.I. of a **circular disc** about an axis:

(a) Through centre and $\perp^r$ to the plane :

$$I = \frac{1}{2}Mr^2.$$

(b) Through a diameter : $I = \frac{1}{4}Mr^2$.

9. M.I. of a **solid sphere** about a diameter :

$$I = \frac{2}{5}Mr^2.$$

10. M.I. of a **hollow sphere** about a diameter :

$$I = \frac{2}{3} Mr^2$$

11. Velocity and acceleration of a body rolling down an inclined plane without slipping:

$$v^2 = \frac{2gh}{1+\left(\frac{K}{r}\right)^2} \text{ and } f = \frac{g\sin\theta}{1+\left(\frac{K}{r}\right)^2}.$$

12. P.E. of a rolling disc or ring $= Mgr$.
13. P.E. of a sphere (solid or hollow) or cylinder $= 0$

Gravity and Gravitation

1. **Gravitational force of attraction (F) in any medium:**

$$F = G\frac{m_1 m_2}{r^2}$$. **Where:** G = universal gravitational constant $= 6.67 \times 10^{-11}$ **S.I. unit.**

2. **Intensity (I) of gravitational field** at a distance r from a body of mass m :

$$I = \frac{Gm}{r^2} = -\frac{dV}{dr}.$$

3. **Gravitational potential** at a point r distance apart from a body of mass m :

$$V = -\frac{Gm}{r}\ .\ [\text{at } \infty,\ V_{max} = 0].$$

4. **Acceleration due to gravity g** on the surface of planet of mass M, radius R and density ρ : $g = \dfrac{Gm}{R^2} = \dfrac{4}{3}\pi G R \rho$.

5. **Variation of g :**

   (a) **Above the surface of the earth at a height h :** $g' = g\dfrac{R^2}{(R+h)^2} \simeq g\left(1 - \dfrac{2h}{R}\right)$.

   (b) **At a depth h below the surface of the earth:** $g' = g\left\{1 - \dfrac{h}{R}\right\}$. At the centre of the earth, $g' = 0$.

   (c) **Due to rotation of the earth:**

$$g' = g\left(1 - \frac{R\omega^2 \cos^2\theta}{g}\right).$$

Where: ω = angular velocity of the earth and θ = latitude.

Special Cases

(*i*) **At pole, $\theta = 90°$, $g' = g$ (maximum)** i.e. maximum weight.

(*ii*) **At equator, $\theta = 0°$,**

$$g' = g\left(1 - \frac{R\omega^2}{g}\right) \text{ minimum.}$$

(*iii*) Difference,

$$g_p - g_e = g - g\left(1 - \frac{R\omega^2}{g}\right) = R\omega^2.$$

(*iv*) Difference in weight of a body at pole and at equator $= mR\omega^2$.

6. **Escape velocity (v_e)**

$$= \sqrt{\frac{2GM}{R}} = \sqrt{2gR} = 7 \text{ miles/sec}$$

= 11.2 km/sec for **Earth.**

(v_e) = 2.4 km/sec for **Moon.**

Where: M = Mass of the planet, R = radius of the planet.

7. **Orbital velocity (v_o)** $= \sqrt{\frac{GM}{R+x}}$ = 5 miles/sec or 8 km/sec for the **Earth.**

Where: x = **distance of the body above earth's surface.**

If $x = 0$ (the satellite is close to the earth),

$$v_0 = \sqrt{\frac{GM}{R}} = \sqrt{gR}\,.$$

8. $v_e = \sqrt{2v_0}$. **N.B.:** v_e **and** v_0 **are independent of the mass of the body.**

9. **Time period of revolution of the satellite (T)**

$$= 2\pi\sqrt{\frac{(R+x)^3}{GM}}\,.$$

If $x = 0$ then $T^2 \propto R^3 \rightarrow$ Kepler's law.

4

HYDROSTATICS

1. **Density (*D*)** $= \frac{M}{V}$.
2. Total thrust (*F*) on the bottom of the vessel: $F = Ah\rho g$.
   Where: A = cross-sectional area of vessel, h = height of liquid column, ρ = density of liquid. [**unit** of $F \rightarrow$ as force].
3. **Pressure (*P*)** $= \frac{\text{total thrust}}{\text{area}} = h\rho g$.
   S.I. unit of P: Pascal or Nm^{-2}, unit of atmospheric pressure = bar.
4. **Specific gravity or relative density (*s*)**
   $$= \frac{\text{density of substance } (\sigma)}{\text{density of } H_2O \text{ at } 4°C (\rho)} \text{ or } \sigma = \rho \times s.$$
   [ρ of H_2O at 4°C in **S.I.** $\rightarrow 10^3$ kg. m^{-3}].

5. **Archimede's principle:** loss in weight = weight of displaced fluid = upward thrust or buoyancy or apparent loss in weight $= W - W_1 = V\rho g$.
Where: W and W_1 = weight of the body in air and in fluid, ρ = density of fluid and V = volume of body immersed.
6. Apparent weight = actual weight – buoyancy

$$= mg - V\rho g = mg \times \frac{m}{\rho'} \times \rho g = mg\left(1 - \frac{\rho}{\rho'}\right),$$

Where: ρ' and ρ = density of solid and fluid.

7. $S = \dfrac{W}{W - W_1}$.

5

HEAT

Thermometry

1. $$\frac{\text{Reading on any scale} - \text{lower fixed point}}{\text{fundamental interval (upper fixed point} - \text{lower fixed point)}}$$

$$= \text{constant or, } \frac{C-0}{100} = \frac{F-32}{180} = \frac{R-0}{80}$$

$$= \frac{K-273}{100} = \frac{Ra-492}{180}.$$

2. **For temperature difference:**

$$\frac{\Delta C}{5} = \frac{\Delta F}{9} = \frac{\Delta R}{4} = \frac{\Delta K}{5} = \frac{\Delta Ra}{9}$$

Expansion of Solids and Liquids

1. $\alpha = \dfrac{l_t - l_0}{l_0 \times t}.$

2. $\beta = \dfrac{S_t - S_0}{S_0 \times t}$.

3. $\gamma = \dfrac{v_t - v_0}{v_0 \times t}$

4. **For an isotropic solid :**

   $\alpha = \dfrac{1}{2}\beta = \dfrac{1}{3}\gamma$ or $\beta = 2\alpha$ and $\gamma = 3\alpha$

5. $\gamma_r = \gamma_a + \gamma_g$. **Where:** γ_r and γ_a = Co-efficient of real and apparant cubical expansion and γ_g = Co-efficient of cubical expansion of glass.

6. $\gamma_r = \dfrac{d_0 - d_t}{d_t \times t}$. **Where:** d_o and d_t = density of liquid at 0°C and t°C.

7. **Weight thermometer:**

   $\gamma_a = \dfrac{m}{M \times t}$. **Where:** m = mass of liquid expelled, M = mass of liquid left and t°C = rise in temperature.

Expansion of Gases and Gas Thermometers

1. **Specific or characteristic gas constant (*R*):** $PV = RT$ for unit mass of gas, and

$R = \frac{R}{M}$. **Where:** M = Molecular weight.

2. **Boltzman constant (K):** $PV = KT$ for one molecule of gas and $K = \frac{R}{N}$.

   Where: N = Avogadro's number.

3. $V_t = V_0(1 + \gamma_p t)$.

   Where: γ_p = volume co-efficient of gas.

4. $P_t = P_0(1 + \gamma_v t)$.

   Where: γ_v = pressure co-efficient of gas.

5. **For ideal gases:** $\gamma_p = \gamma_v = \frac{1}{273}$ per °C or $\frac{1}{491.4}$ per °F.

6. $T_B = \frac{27}{8} T_C$.

   Where: T_B = Boyle temperature and T_C = critical temperature.

7. **Vanderwaal's equation for real gases :**

$$\left(P + \frac{a}{V^2}\right)(V - b) = RT.$$

8. **Constant volume gas thermometer:**

$$t = \frac{P_t - P_0}{P_{100} - P_0} \times 100° \text{C}.$$

9. **Platinum resistance thermometer:**

$$t = \frac{R_t - R_0}{R_{100} - R_0} \times 100° \text{C}.$$

10. **Callender's compensated constant pressure air thermometer :**

$$t = \frac{W_R}{W - W_R} \times 273° \text{C}.$$

Where: W = weight of Hg required to fill up the reservoir and W_R = weight of Hg taken out for equalising pressure.

Calorimetry

1. **Units of heat energy :**
   (*i*) **S.I.** → Joule.
   (*ii*) **C.G.S** → calorie.
   (*iii*) **F.P.S** → B.T.U., THERM, C.H.U.
   Relations: 1 THERM = 10^5 B.T.U., 1 B.T.U. = 252 cals.,

   1 C.H.U. = 453.6 cals., 1 Joule = $\frac{1}{4.2}$ cals.

2. **Specific heat capacity or specific heat (s):** $Q = ms\theta$.
   S.I. unit of (s) = $Jkg^{-1}K^{-1}$. [Relative specific heat has no unit].
3. **Thermal capacity or heat capacity** = ms.
   S.I. unit: JK^{-1}.
4. **Water equivalent (W)** = ms. **S.I. unit** → **kg.**
5. **Latent heat of fusion (L)**

$$= \frac{Q}{m} = 80 \text{ cal/gm} = 3.35 \times 10^5 \text{ J/kg (for ice)}.$$

6. **Latent heat of vaporisation (L)**

$$= \frac{Q}{m} = 540 \text{ cal/gm} = 2260 \times 10^3 \text{ J/kg (for}$$

water).

7. **For any liquid:** $L = L_i + L_e$. **Where:** L_i and L_e = Internal and external latent heat.
8. **Rate of cooling** = $\frac{\theta_1 - \theta_2}{t} = K(\theta_m - \theta_0)$.

   In terms of calculus

$$= -\frac{d(\theta_1 - \theta_2)}{dt} = -\frac{d\theta}{dt} = K(\theta_m - \theta_0) = K\theta$$

Where: $K = \dfrac{A}{ms}$ for a given body, t = time in which temperature falls from θ_1 to θ_2, θ_m = mean temperature during the time interval t and θ_0 = temperature of surrounding.

Specific Heat of Gases, Isothermal and Adiabatic Changes

1. $C_p - C_v = \dfrac{R}{J}$. **Where:** R in erg or Joule.

   $C_p - C_v = R$ When R in calorie.

2. $\dfrac{C_p}{C_v} = \gamma$ (always > 1). **S.I. unit of** C_p **and** C_v $=$ Joule mole^{-1} K^{-1}.
3. $\gamma = 1.66$, 1.41 and 1.33 for mono, di and tri-atomic gases.
4. **For adiabatic changes:**

   (*i*) $PV^{\gamma} = K$. (*ii*) $TV^{\gamma-1} = K$.

   (*iii*) $T^{\gamma}P^{1-\gamma} = K$.

   Where: K = constant

5. Work done by a gas during:

(*i*) isothermal (for 1 mole) :

$$W = RT \log_e \frac{V_2}{V_1}.$$

(*ii*) adiabatic (for 1 mole) :

$$W = \frac{R}{\gamma - 1}(T_1 - T_2) = \frac{1}{\gamma - 1}(P_1V_1 - P_2V_2).$$

Mechanical Equivalent of Heat, Transmission of Heat and Hygrometry

1. $J = \frac{W}{H}.$

Where: W = mechanical work, H = equivalent heat and J = mechanical equivalent of heat $\simeq$ 4.2 Joule/cal.

In S.I. $\rightarrow$ W and H in Joule, hence $J = 1$ and $W = H$.

2. In steady state, amount of heat flown in time t:

$$Q = KA \frac{\theta_2 - \theta_1}{l} t.$$

Where: $(\theta_2 - \theta_1)$ = difference of temperature over length l, A = cross-sectional area, K = co-efficient of thermal conductivity.

N.B.: $\frac{KA}{l}$ = thermal conductance and

$\frac{l}{KA}$ = thermal resistance.

S.I. unit of $K = \text{Js}^{-1}\,\text{m}^{-1}\,{}^\circ\text{K}^{-1}$ or watt $\text{m}^{-1}\,{}^\circ\text{K}^{-1}$

3. **Ingen hauz's experiment:**

$$\frac{K_1}{l_1^2} = \frac{K_2}{l_2^2} = \frac{K_3}{l_3^2} = \ldots\ldots\ldots = \text{constant}.$$

4. $h = \frac{K}{\rho s}$.

Where: h = thermometric conductivity of diffusivity and ρs = thermal capacity volume.

5. **Stefan's law:** $E = \sigma T^4$.
   Where: σ = stefan's constant.
6. **Wein's displacement law:**

$$\lambda_m \times T = \text{constant}.$$

7. Relative humidity

$$= \frac{\text{saturated vapour pressure at dew point}}{\text{saturated vapour pressure at air temperature}} \times 100\%$$

$$= \frac{\text{saturated vapour pressure at dew point}}{\text{saturated vapour pressure at } t^\circ\text{C of air}} \times 100\%$$

6

SOUND

Speed, Reflection, Refraction and Beats

1. $v = n\lambda$.
2. $n = \frac{1}{T}$. **Unit of** n : 1 cps = 1 hertz.
3. Distance travelled by the wave = number of vibrations × λ.
4. **Normal hearing range → 20 cps to 20×10^3 cps.**
5. **MACH Number** $= \frac{\text{speed of the body}}{\text{speed of sound}}$.
6. Speed of any longitudinal wave in any medium : $v = \sqrt{\frac{E}{\rho}}$.

   Where: E = elasticity, ρ = density of the medium.

7. Speed in solid, $v_s = \sqrt{\frac{\gamma}{\rho}}$.

Where: γ **= Young's modulus.**

8. Speed in liquid $v_l = \sqrt{\frac{K}{\rho}}$.

Where: K **= Bulk modulus.**

9. According to **Laplace:** $v = \sqrt{\frac{\gamma p}{\rho}} = C\sqrt{\frac{\gamma}{3}}$.

Where: $\gamma = \frac{C_p}{C_v}$, C = R.M.S. velocity and

γp = adiabatic elasticity, v_{air} at N.T.P. = 332 m/sec = 1120 ft/sec.

10. $\frac{v_t}{v_0} = \sqrt{\frac{T}{T_0}}$.

11. $v = \frac{2d}{t}$. **Where:** d = distance of reflector.

12. Number of beats/sec = $n_1 - n_2$. i.e. difference in frequency.

N.B.: Interference as in the case of light wave.

Laws of Transverse Vibrations of String and Organ Pipe

1. $n = \frac{p}{2l}\sqrt{\frac{T}{m}}$, if the wire vibrates in p loop.

   If $p = 1$, then $n_1 = \frac{1}{2l}\sqrt{\frac{T}{m}}$, fundamental tone or 1st harmonic.

   If $p = 2$, then $n_2 = \frac{2}{2l}\sqrt{\frac{T}{m}}$, 1st overtone or 2nd harmonic.

2. $n \propto \frac{1}{r}$. [l, T and ρ constant]

3. $n \propto \frac{1}{\sqrt{\rho}}$. [$l$, T and r constant]

4. (*i*) $\lambda = 2l$, for single loop vibration.

   (*ii*) $\lambda = \frac{2l}{p}$, for p loop vibration.

5. **Velocity of any transverse wave in a medium:**

$v = \sqrt{\frac{T}{m}}$, whether wire vibrates in a single loop or p loops.

Symbols used above: T = tension, m = mass per unit length, l = length, r = radius, ρ = density and n = frequency.

6. **Fundamental frequency of the closed organ's pipe :** $n_1 = \frac{v}{4l}$.
7. **Fundamental frequency of open organ's pipe:** $n_2 = \frac{v}{2l} = 2\left(\frac{v}{4l}\right) = 2n_1$.
8. **Other frequencies :**

   (a) **Closed pipe:** 1st overtone = $3n_1$ = 2nd harmonic, 2nd overtone = $5n_1$ =3rd harmonic.

   (b) **Open pipe:** 1st overtone = $2n_2$ = 2nd harmonic, 2nd overtone = $3n_2$ = 3rd harmonic, 3rd overtone = $4n_2$ = 4th harmonics.

9. Diameter $\propto \lambda \propto \frac{l}{n}$, when length of the pipe is constant.
10. Effective lenth $= l + 0.6r$, Where: r = radius, l = length.

Qualities of Musical Sound and Vibration of Bars

1. **Interval** $= \frac{n_1}{n_2}$. $[n_1 \geq n_2]$.
2. **Unision,** If $n_1 = n_2$; **Octave,** If $n_1 = 2n_2$.
3. **For plane sound waves :** $I = 2\pi^2 a^2 n^2 \rho v$,

   also $I \propto \frac{1}{r^2}$.

   Where: I = intensity, a = amplitude, n = frequency, ρ = density of the medium, v = velocity of sound and r = distance of listner. **Unit of** $(I) \rightarrow$ watt/m^2.
   1 Bel (B) = 10 deci Bel (dB),
   Phon = dB at $n = 10^3$ Hz.
4. **Determination of pitch (frequency)**
   (a) **Siren plate method:** $N = m \times n$.

Where: N = frequency, n = number of revolutions/sec, m = number of holes.

(b) **Stroboscopic method:** $N = \frac{1}{2} m \times n$

(c) **Falling plate method:**

$$N = \frac{\text{number of waves}}{\sqrt{\frac{2s}{g}}} = \frac{\text{number of waves}}{\sqrt{\frac{l_2 - l_1}{g}}}.$$

5. **Frequency of Tuning fork:** $n = \frac{m^2 K}{2\pi l^2} \sqrt{\frac{\gamma}{\rho}}$.

Where: m = a constant = 1.875, $K = a \times \sqrt{12}$

Where: a = thickness of prong, l = length of prong, ρ = density of the fork.

N.B.: Doppler's Effect: Same as shown by light wave.

7

MAGNETISM

Pole Strength, Intensity, Induction and Potential

1. **Magnetic pole strength,** $m = i\Delta l \sin\theta$, or $[m] = [IL]$.
2. **Coulomb's law: In S.I. unit →**

$$F = \frac{\mu_0\mu_r}{4\pi} \times \frac{m_1 m_2}{r^2} = \frac{\mu}{4\pi} \times \frac{m_1 m_2}{r^2}$$ in a homogeneous medium.

For air or vacuum $\mu_r = 1$, hence

$$F = \frac{\mu_0}{4\pi} \times \frac{m_1 m_2}{r^2}.$$

Where: μ_0 = permeability of vacuum, μ_r = relative permeability of the medium (no unit) and $\mu = \mu_0\,\mu_r$ = permeability indicates power of medium to conduct magnetic flux.

In S.I. system, $\mu_0 = 4\pi \times 10^{-7}$ weber/amp × m or henry/m or N/m^2.

3. The **magnetic induction** (B) due to single pole of strength m, at a distance r from it:

$$B = \frac{\mu_0 \mu_r}{4\pi} \cdot \frac{m}{r^2}$$. In vacuum or air $B = \frac{\mu_0 m}{4\pi r^2}$,

$(\because \mu_r = 1)$.

4. A pole of strength m, amp × m in field of magnetic induction B weber/m^2, experiences a force of mB newton, i.e. $\vec{F} = m\vec{B}$.

For n-pole (m = + ve), $\vec{F} \parallel \vec{B}$. For s-pole (m = –ve), $\vec{F} \parallel -\vec{B}$.

5. $B = \mu H = \mu_0 \mu_r H$. **Where:** H = auxiliary field or intensity of magnetic field. For a single pole of strength m; H at a distance r:

$$H = \frac{1}{4\pi} \times \frac{m}{r^2}$$ (independent of the surrounding).

6. $\phi = \vec{B}.\vec{A}$ or $\phi = AB\cos\alpha$. **Where:** $\vec{A}$ = area vector, $\vec{B}$ = magnetic induction vector, ϕ = magnetic flux and α = angle between $\vec{B}$ and normal to area $\vec{A}$.

7. **Magnetic potential** (V) at a point at a distance r from a magnetic pole of strength m: $V = \frac{\mu}{4\pi}\left(\frac{m}{r}\right) = \frac{\mu_0\mu_r}{4\pi}\left(\frac{m}{r}\right)$.

8. $B = -\frac{dV}{dr}$

9. $M = m \times 2l$. **Where:** M = magnetic dipole moment, $2l$ = separation between poles and m = pole strength.

10. **Potential and magnetic induction due to a dipole:**

 (i) The **magnetic potential** (V) at a point (r, θ) at a distance r from the dipole and making an angle θ with dipole moment

(M) : $V = \frac{\mu}{4\pi} \cdot \frac{M\cos\theta}{r^2}$. If $\theta = 0°$,

$V = \frac{\mu}{4\pi} \times \frac{M}{r^2}$ (on the axis of dipole),

If $\theta = 90°$, $V = 0$, (at right angles to the axis).

(ii) **Magnetic induction** due to a dipole at a point (r, θ):

$B = \frac{\mu_0 \mu_r}{4\pi} \cdot \frac{M}{r^3} \times \sqrt{1 + 3\cos^2\theta}$ and

$\tan\alpha = \frac{\tan\theta}{2}$, If B makes an angle $\beta = (\alpha + \theta)$ with dipole moment.

(a) If $\theta = 0°$ or $180°$, $B = \frac{\mu}{4\pi} \cdot \frac{2M}{r^3}$,

$\alpha = 0°$, $\beta = 0°$ and $\vec{B}$ is in the direction of $\vec{M} (\vec{B} \parallel \vec{M})$.

(b) If $\theta = 90°$, $B = \frac{\mu}{4\pi} \cdot \frac{M}{r^3}$, $\alpha = 90°$,

$\beta = 180°$ and $\vec{B}$ is opposite to $\vec{M}(\vec{B} \parallel -\vec{M})$.

11. The **moment of couple** ($\vec{\tau}$) of a magnetic dipole in uniform magnetic field $= MB \sin\theta$;

$(\vec{\tau} = \vec{M} \times \vec{B})$.

12. **Potential energy** (W) of a magnetic dipole in uniform magnetic field : $W = MB(1 - \cos\theta)$.

Special conditions :

(a) If $\theta = 0°$, $W = 0$ (minimum).

(b) If $\theta = 90°$, $W = MB$

(c) If $\theta = 180°$, $W = 2MB$ (maximum).

13. **Magnetic field induction (B) due to a bar magnet:**

(a) **End-on position** (point-on axis of magnet): $B = \frac{\mu}{4\pi}\left(\frac{2Md}{(d^2 - l^2)^2}\right)$, $\vec{B} \parallel \vec{M}$.

Where: d = distance of point from the centre of a bar magnet.

In vacuum or air, $B = \frac{\mu_0}{4\pi} \times \frac{2Md}{(d^2 - l^2)^2}$

and $H = \frac{1}{4\pi} \times \frac{2Md}{(d^2 - l^2)^2}$.

For a **short magnet** in vacuum or air :

$$B = \frac{\mu_0}{4\pi} \times \frac{2M}{d^3}, \ \vec{B} \parallel \vec{M}, \ (\because l << d).$$

(b) **Broad-side-on position** (point on $\perp^r$ bisector):

$$B' = \frac{\mu}{4\pi}\left(\frac{M}{(d^2 + l^2)^{\frac{3}{2}}}\right), \ \vec{B'} \parallel -\vec{M}.$$

$$B' = \frac{\mu_0}{4\pi}\left(\frac{M}{(d^2 + l^2)^{\frac{3}{2}}}\right), \text{ for vacuum or air.}$$

$B' = \frac{\mu_0}{4\pi}\left(\frac{M}{d^3}\right)$, $\vec{B'} \parallel -\vec{M}$. For a **short magnet** in air ($l << d$).

14. **Intensity of magnetization** $(I) = \frac{M}{V} = \frac{m}{A}$.

Magnetometry

1. **Gauss tangent law:**

   $B = B_H \tan\theta, (B \perp^r B_H)$.

2. **TanA - position (of gauss):**

   $$B = \frac{\mu}{4\pi}\left(\frac{2Md}{(d^2 - l^2)^2}\right) = B_H \tan\theta.$$

   For a short magnet:

   $$B = \frac{\mu}{4\pi}\left(\frac{2M}{d^3}\right) = B_H \tan\theta$$

3. **TanB - position (of gauss):**

   $$B = \frac{\mu}{4\pi}\left(\frac{M}{(d^2 + l^2)^{\frac{3}{2}}}\right) = B_H \tan\theta.$$

   For a short magnet: $B = \frac{\mu}{4\pi}\left(\frac{M}{d^3}\right) = B_H \tan\theta$

4. **Oscillation magnetometer:** In uniform magnetic field of magnetic induction (B), **time period,**

$$T = 2\pi\sqrt{\frac{I}{MB}} \text{ or } T = 2\pi\sqrt{\frac{I}{MB+C}}.$$

Where: C = couple per unit radian twist.

For a **bar magnet:** $I = W\dfrac{l^2+b^2}{12}$.

Where: W = mass.

5. **For a given oscillating magnet:**

$$\frac{n_1}{n_2} = \sqrt{\frac{B_1}{B_2}}, \text{ i.e. } n \propto \sqrt{B}.$$

Where: n = frequency.

6. **Comparision of magnetic moments of two magnets using them simultaneously:**

$$\frac{M_1}{M_2} = \frac{T_2^2 + T_1^2}{T_2^2 - T_1^2} = \frac{n_1^2 + n_2^2}{n_1^2 - n_2^2}.$$

Terrestrial Magnetism

1. $\tan\delta = \dfrac{B_V}{B_H}$.

2. $B_E = \sqrt{B_H^2 + B_V^2}$.

   Where: δ = angle of dip or inclination.

3. **Apparent angle of dip** (δ_1) in a vertical plane making an angle (θ) with magnetic meridian: $\tan\delta_1 = \dfrac{\tan\delta}{\cos\theta}$.

   Where: δ = true angle of dip.

4. Value of the **true dip** (δ) from the measurement of apparent dips (δ_1 and δ_2) at a place : $\cot^2\delta = \cot^2\delta_1 + \cot^2\delta_2$.

Properties of Magnetic Materials

1. $K = \dfrac{I}{H}$ (no unit) .

2. $\mu = \dfrac{B}{H}$ (no unit in **CGS emu.**).

3. $B = \mu_0(H + I)$.

4. $\mu_r = 1 + K$.

5. $\mu = 1 + 4\pi K$ **(CGS).**

6. In **S.I.** : $\mu = \mu_0\mu_r$. (μ has same unit as μ_0).

   Where: K = susceptibility and I = intensity of magnetization.

UNITS OF MAGNETIC VARIABLES

Variables with nature and symbol	S.I. Unit	C. G. S e. m. u.	Relation
1. Magnetic strength (m) **(scalar)**	ampere × metre (am)	e.m.u. of m or ab amp × cm	1 am = 10 e.m.u of m
2. Magnetic moment ($\vec{M}$) **(vector)**	amp × m^2 or joule/tesla	e.m.u of moment	1 $am^2 = 10^3$ e.m.u of moment
3. Magnetic flux (ϕ) **(scalar)**	weber (wb)	maxwell or gauss cm^2	1 wb = 10^8 maxwell
4. Magnetic potential (V) **(scalar)**	joule/am	e.m.u of potential	1 joule/am $=10^6$ e.m.u of potential
5. Magnetic induction ($\vec{B}$) **(vector)**	weber/m^2 or newton/am or tesla	gauss	1wb/m^2 $=10^4$ gauss
6. Auxiliary field or intensity of magnetic field (H) **(vector)**	amp/metre (am^{-1})	oersted	1 $am^{-1} = 4\pi \times 10^{-3}$ oersted
7. Intensity of magnetisation (I) **(vector)**	amp/metre (am^{-1})	gauss	1 $am^{-1} = 10^{-3}$ gauss

8

ELECTROSTATICS

Electric Charge

1. $Q = ne.$

2. **Surface charge density (σ) = $\frac{Q}{A}$.**

3. **Volume density of charge (ρ) = $\frac{Q}{V}$.**

   N.B.: For spherical conductor $\rightarrow A = 4\pi r^2$

   and $V = \frac{4}{3}\pi r^3$.

4. **Coulomb's law: In C.G.S:** $F = \frac{Q_1 Q_2}{Kr^2}$.

   In S.I. : $F = \frac{1}{4\pi \in_0 \in_r} \times \frac{Q_1 Q_2}{r^2}$

   $= \frac{1}{4\pi \in} \times \frac{Q_1 Q_2}{r^2}$ in homogeneous medium.

Where: K = dielectric constant of the medium or specific inductive capacity, ϵ_0 = absolute permitivity of the free space (air or vacuum), ϵ_r = relative permitivity of the medium (no unit, for air or vacuum, $\epsilon_r = 1$) and $\epsilon = \epsilon_0 \epsilon_r$ = absolute permitivity of the dielectric or medium,

$$\epsilon_0 = \frac{1}{36\pi \times 10^9} = 8.85 \times 10^{-12} \frac{\text{coul}^2}{N \times m^2} = \frac{\text{farad}}{\text{meter}} \text{ and } 4\pi\,\epsilon_0 = \frac{1}{9 \times 10^9} \frac{\text{coul}^2}{N \times m^2}$$

$$= \frac{\text{farad}}{\text{meter}}.$$

5. E (vector) $= \dfrac{Q}{4\pi\,\epsilon_0 \epsilon_r\, r^2}$ in homogeneous medium.

Where: E = intensity of electric field

$$E = \frac{1}{4\pi\,\epsilon_0} \cdot \frac{Q}{r^2} \text{ (in air).}$$

6. $V = \dfrac{1}{4\pi\,\epsilon_0 \epsilon_r} \times \dfrac{Q}{r}$ in homogeneous medium.

7. $E = -\frac{dv}{dx}$. **Where:** $\frac{dv}{dx}$ is potential gradient.
8. **Force** (F) on a charge q at a point where electric field intensity is $E : F = q.E$.
9. **Work done** (ΔW) in moving a charge Q between two points having a P.D. ΔV by any path: $\Delta W = Q\Delta V$.
10. **Electric displacement** (D) (vector)

$$= \in E = \frac{Q}{4\pi r^2}.$$

11. $d\phi = E.ds \cos\theta$. **In vector form** : $d\phi = \vec{E}.d\vec{s}$.
Where: $d\phi$ = electric flux (scalar), ds = small element of surface surrounding the point, θ = angle made by normal to ds to the direction of E.
12. **Mutual electric potential energy (U):**

(*i*) $U = \frac{1}{4\pi \in}.\frac{Q_1Q_2}{r}$, when both Q_1 and Q_2 are +ve.

(*ii*) $U = -\frac{1}{4\pi \in}.\frac{Q_1Q_2}{r}$ if one of the charges is, –ve.

Electric Dipole

1. **Dipole moment** (vector) = electric charge × distance between them, i.e. $P = q \times 2l$.
   S.I. unit → coul × m.
   Special unit → Debye. 1 Debye = 1D
   $= \frac{1}{3} \times 10^{-29}$ coul × meter.

2. Electric **potential and intensity** at a point r distance apart, making an angle θ with dipole moment vector:

   $$V = \frac{1}{4\pi \in} \times \frac{P \cos\theta}{r^2},$$

   $$E = \frac{P}{4\pi \in r^3} \times \sqrt{1 + 3\cos^2\theta}.$$

   If α be the angle between $\vec{E}$ and $\vec{r}$, then

   $\tan\alpha = \frac{1}{2}\tan\theta$.

   If β be the angle between $\vec{E}$ and $\vec{r}$, then $\beta = (\alpha + \theta)$.

3. **Special cases:**
   (*i*) If the point be on the **axis of dipole**, i.e. $\theta = 0°$ or $180°$;

$$V_1 = \frac{\pm P}{4\pi \in r^2} \text{ and } E_1 = \frac{2P}{4\pi \in r^3}, (\vec{E}_1 || \vec{P})$$

(*ii*) If the point be on $\perp^r$ **bisector**, i.e. $\theta = 90°$ or $270°$;

$$V_2 = 0 \text{ and } E_2 = \frac{P}{4\pi \in r^3}, (\vec{E}_2 || -\vec{P}).$$

4. **P.E. of an electric dipole in an electric field:**
   $U = PE(1 - \cos\theta)$ Joule. **Where:** θ = angle between $\vec{P}$ and $\vec{E}$.

5. **Binding energy of the dipole** $= \frac{1}{4\pi \in} \cdot \frac{q^2}{r}$.

6. **Torque** $(\vec{\tau})$ acting on a dipole in uniform electric field :

   $\vec{\tau} = \vec{P} \times \vec{E}$ or $\vec{\tau} = PE \sin\theta$.

   Where: θ = angle between $\vec{P}$ and $\vec{E}$.

7. **Electric flux** (ϕ) $= E\,\Delta s \cos\theta$.
   Where: θ = angle between the direction of E and normal to the area Δs.

In vector form: $\phi = \vec{E} \times \Delta \vec{s}$.
S.I. unit = volt × m or $N \times m^2$/coul.

Capacity and Condensers

1. $C = \dfrac{Q}{V}$.

2. **Capacity** of a sphere of radius r in a homogeneous medium of permitivity $\in$:
   In S.I. : $C = 4\pi \in r = 4\pi \in_0 \in_r r$.
   In air $\in_r = 1$, $\therefore C_a = 4\pi \in_0 r$ (minimum).
   In medium $C_m = 4\pi \in_0 \in_r r = C_a \in_r$,

   $\therefore$ **In S.I.:** $C = \in_r = \dfrac{C_m}{C_a}$.

3. $W = \dfrac{1}{2} CV^2 = \dfrac{1}{2} QV = \dfrac{Q^2}{2C}$ Joule.

   Where: W = electrostatic potential energy of charged conductor.

4. **In sharing of charges between two conductors:**

   (*i*) $V = \dfrac{Q_1 + Q_2}{C_1 + C_2} = \dfrac{C_1 V_1 + C_2 V_2}{C_1 + C_2}$.

(*ii*) **Loss of energy**

$$= \Delta W = \frac{1}{2}\left(\frac{C_1C_2}{C_1+C_2}\right)(V_1 - V_2)^2$$

(*iii*) **For no energy loss:** $V_1 = V_2$. [ΔW is always + ve].

5. **Parallel plate condenser with simple dielectric : In S.I.**

(*i*) $C = \frac{\epsilon A}{d}$. (*ii*) $E = \frac{\sigma}{\epsilon}$. (*iii*) $V = Ed = \frac{\sigma d}{\epsilon}$.

(*iv*) $Q = A\sigma = CV$.

(*v*) $W = \frac{1}{2}CV^2 = \frac{1}{2}QV = \frac{Q^2}{2C}$.

Where: A = area of each of the plates d = distance between the plates.

6. **Parallel plate condenser with compound dielectric:**

$$C = \frac{A}{\frac{d-t}{\epsilon_0} + \frac{t}{\epsilon_0\epsilon_r}} = \frac{A}{\Sigma\frac{d}{\epsilon}}.$$

Where: t = thickness of insulating medium.

7. **Spherical condenser : In S.I. :**

$$C = 4\pi \in \frac{r_2 r_1}{r_2 - r_1}.$$

Where: r_1 = radius of inner sphere, r_2 = radius of outer sphere (earthed) and $r_2 - r_1$ = thickness of insulating material.

8. **Cylindrical condenser : In S.I. :**

$$C = \frac{2\pi \in l}{\log e \frac{r_2}{r_1}}; (r_1 < r_2).$$

Where: l = length of either cylinder, r_1 = radius of inner cylinder and r_2 = radius of outer cylinder.

9. **Capacity of Leyden Jar : In S.I. :**

$$C = 4\pi \in -\frac{r^2 + 2rh}{4d}.$$

Where: r = radius of jar, h = height of plate, d = thickness of glass wall.

10. **In series:** $\frac{1}{C} = \frac{1}{C_1} + \frac{1}{C_2} + \frac{1}{C_3} + ...$

11. **In parallel:** $C = C_1 + C_2 + C_3 + ...$

UNITS OF ELECTROSTATICS VARIABLES

Physical quantity with symbol and nature	**S.I. Unit**	**C.G.S. (e.s.u.)**	**Relation**
1. Charge (Q) **(scalar)**	coulomb (C)	stat coul or e.s.u	1 coul = 3×10^9 stat coul
2. Surface density of charge (σ) **(scalar)**	coul/m^2	stat coul/ cm^2	1 coul/m^2 = 3×10^5 stat coul/cm^2
3. Intensity of electric field (E) **(vector)**	volt/m or newton/ coul	stat volt/ cm	1 stat volt/cm = 3×10^4 volt/m
4. Electric potential (V) **(scalar)**	volt or joule/coul	stat volt erg/ stat coul	1 stat volt = 300 volt
5. Electric displacement (D) **(vector)**	coul/m^2	stat coul/ cm^2	1 coul/m^2 = 3×10^5 stat coul/ cm^2
6. Electric flux (ϕ) **(scalar)**	Nm^2/coul or volt × meter	stat volt cm	1 volt m = 1/3 stat volt × cm
7. Electrostatic potential energy (U) **(scalar)**	joule	erg	1 joule = 10^7 ergs
8. Electrostatic stress on a charged conductor **(vector)**	newton/ m^2	dyne/cm^2	1 newton/m^2 = 10 dynes/cm^2

9. Dipole moment (ρ) **(vector)**	coul × m	stat coul × cm	1 coul × m = 3×10^{11} stat coul × cm
10. Torque (τ) **(vector)**	newton×m	dyne×cm	1 N × m = 10^7 dyne × cm
11. Capacity (*C*) **(scalar)**	farad or coul/volt	stat-farad or e.s.u of *C*.	1 farad = 9 × 10^{11} stat farad

9

LIGHT

Plane Mirrors

1. $\frac{1}{v}+\frac{1}{u}=\frac{1}{f}=\frac{1}{\infty}=0, m=1$.

2. **Deviation of ray:**

   (*i*) **On single reflection:**
   $D=\pi-2i=180^\circ-2i.$

   (*ii*) **On successive reflections :**
   $D=2(\pi-\theta)=360^\circ-2\theta.$

3. **Number of images formed in two inclined mirror:**

   (*i*) If $\frac{360}{\theta}=\text{odd}, n=\frac{360}{\theta}, n=\frac{360}{\theta}-1$, for object exactly midway.

   (*ii*) If $\frac{360}{\theta}=\text{even}, n=\frac{360}{\theta}-1.$

(*iii*) If $\frac{360}{\theta}$ = fraction, n = next whole number.

Spherical Mirrors

Formulae are based on cartesian co-ordinate axes sign convention.

1. According to this sign convention:
   (*i*) **For real image by concave** (converging) **mirror:** $u = -$ ve, $v = -$ve, $f = -$ve and $r = -$ve.
   (*ii*) **For virtual image by concave mirror:** $u = -$ ve, $v = +$ve, $f = -$ve and $r = -$ve.
   (*iii*) **For virtual image by convex** (diverging) **mirror:** $u = -$ ve, $v = +$ve, $f = +$ve and $r = +$ve.
2. **For spherical mirrors of small aperture:**

   for axial rays : $\frac{1}{v} + \frac{1}{u} = \frac{1}{f} = \frac{2}{r}$.

   For non-axial rays: $\frac{1}{v} + \frac{1}{u} = \frac{2\cos i}{r}$.
3. **Linear or transverse magnification (*M*):**

$$M = \frac{\text{size of image}}{\text{size of object}} = \frac{v}{u} = \frac{v-f}{f} = \frac{f}{u-f} = \frac{v-r}{u-r}.$$

4. **Surface magnification** $= \dfrac{v^2}{u^2}$.

5. **Longitudinal or axial magnification (L):**

$$= \frac{v^2}{u^2} = M^2.$$

6. **Newton's formula:** $u.v = f^2$
Where: u and v are distance of object and image respectively, from the focus.

7. **Angular magnification** $= -\dfrac{1}{M}$.

Where: $M = \dfrac{v}{u}$.

Refraction at Plane Surface

1. $\mu = \dfrac{C_0}{C_m} = \dfrac{\lambda_0}{\lambda_m}$.

Where: μ = refractive index of a medium.

2. $^{a}\mu_b = \dfrac{\text{R.I. of medium } b}{\text{R.I. of medium } a} = \dfrac{\text{velocity of light in } a}{\text{velocity of light in } b}$

3. ${}^a\mu_b \times {}^b\mu_a = 1$ and ${}^a\mu_b = \frac{1}{{}^b\mu_a}$.

4. **Light passing through different media:**

   (i) ${}^a\mu_b \times {}^b\mu_c \times {}^c\mu_a = {}^a\mu_a = 1.$

   (ii) ${}^a\mu_b \times {}^b\mu_c = {}^a\mu_c$.

5. **Snell's law** : For same colour of light :

   ${}^a\mu_b = \frac{\sin i}{\sin r}$, $[i \neq 0]$.

   Generalised: $\mu_1 \sin\phi_1 = \mu_2 \sin\phi_2 = \ldots\ldots\ldots = \mu_n \sin\phi_n$.

6. Cauchy's formula: $\mu = A + \frac{B}{\lambda^2}$.

   Where: A and B are cauchy's constant.

7. Refraction through plane parallel plates:
   Lateral displacement (D) = $t \sec r \sin(i - r)$
   Where: t = slab's thickness.

8. **Object in denser and observer in rarer medium:**

   (i) $\frac{\mu_2}{\mu_1} = \frac{\text{real depth}}{\text{apparent depth}}$.

Where: μ_2 = R.I. of denser medium
μ_1 = R.I. of rarer medium.

(*ii*) $\mu = \frac{t}{d} = \frac{t}{t-x}$ or $x = \frac{t(\mu-1)}{\mu}$.

Where: d = apparent position.

(*iii*) $d = \frac{t_1}{\mu_1} + \frac{t_2}{\mu_2} + \ldots\ldots\ldots\ldots + \frac{t_n}{\mu_n} = \Sigma \frac{t}{\mu}$.

9. **Object in rarer medium and observer in denser medium:**

$$\frac{\mu_2}{\mu_1} = \frac{\text{apparent depth}}{\text{real depth}}.$$

10. **Total internal reflection :** $\frac{\mu_1}{\mu_2} = \sin C$.

Where: μ_1 = R.I. of rarer medium and μ_2 = R.I. of denser medium.

If $\mu_1 = 1$ (for vacuum); $\mu_2 = \frac{1}{\sin C}$.

Where: C = critical angle.

11. **Vision of a fish or a diver:**

$$r = \frac{h}{\sqrt{\mu^2 - 1}}.$$

Prism, Combination of Prisms, Spectra

1. $D = i + i' - A$.
   Where: i = angle of incidence, i' = angle of emergence and A = refracting angle of prism.
2. $A = r + r'$.
   Where: r = angle of refraction at the 1st surface and r' = angle of refraction at the second surface.
3. **For minimum deviation:** $i = i'$ and $r = r'$
   $\therefore D_m = 2i - A$.
4. $A_{max} = 2C$.
   Where: C = critical angle.
5. For a thin prism: $D_m = A(\mu - 1)$.
6. Minimum angle of incidence (i_{min}) for a light ray to pass through a prism:

   $$\sin i_{min} = \sin A\sqrt{\mu^2 - 1 - \cos A}\,.$$
7. **Angular dispersion (β)**
   $= D_v - D_r = A(\mu_v - \mu_r)$.
   Where: D_v and D_r = deviation for violet and red ray, μ_v and μ_r = R.I. for violet and red ray.

8. **Dispersive power (ω)**

$$= \frac{\text{angular dispersion}}{\text{mean deviation}} = \frac{D_v - D_r}{D_y} = \frac{\mu_v - \mu_r}{\mu_y - 1}$$

Where: D_y = deviation for mean yellow colour. μ_y = R.I. of mean yellow colour.

9. **Dispersion without deviation:**

(*i*) $\frac{\mu' - 1}{\mu - 1} = -\frac{A}{A'}$.

(*ii*) **Total dispersion** $= A(\mu - 1)(\omega - \omega')$.

10. **Deviation without dispersion:**

(*i*) $\frac{\mu_v' - \mu_r'}{\mu_v - \mu_r} = -\frac{A}{A'}$

(*ii*) **Total deviation of the mean ray**

$$= A(\mu - 1)\left(1 - \frac{\omega}{\omega'}\right).$$

Refraction of light at spherical surfaces, lenses and defects of vision

1. Refraction at a single spherical surface (small aperture):

$$\frac{\mu_2}{v} - \frac{\mu_1}{u} = \frac{\mu_2 - \mu_1}{r}.$$

2. **Sign convention:**
   (*i*) **For real image by convex** (converging) **lens:** $u = -\text{ve}$, $v = +\text{ve}$, $f = +\text{ve}$, $P = +\text{ve}$.
   (*ii*) **For virtual image by convex lens:** $u = -\text{ve}$, $v = -\text{ve}$, $f = +\text{ve}$, $P = +\text{ve}$.
   (*iii*) **For virtual image by concave** (diverging) **lens:** $u = -\text{ve}$, $v = -\text{ve}$, $f = -\text{ve}$, $P = -\text{ve}$.
3. **For thin lenses:**

$$\frac{1}{v} - \frac{1}{u} = \frac{1}{f} = \left(\frac{\mu_2}{\mu_1} - 1\right)\left(\frac{1}{r_1} - \frac{1}{r_2}\right).$$

   Where: μ_2 and μ_1 = R. I. of lens material and surrounding medium.
4. **Linear or lateral or transverse magnification (*m*) :**

$$m = \frac{\text{size of image } (I)}{\text{size of object } (O)} = \frac{v}{u}.$$

5. **Power of a lens** $(P) = \frac{1}{f}$.

   Where: P in diopter, f in metres; $P = \frac{100}{f}$.

   Where : f in centimeter.

6. **Combination of lenses :**

(*i*) $P = P_1 + P_2 + P_3 + \ldots\ldots\ldots$

(*ii*) $P = P_1 + P_2$ (in case of two lenses).

(*iii*) If two thin lenses are separated by a distance (d) $\frac{1}{f} = \frac{1}{f_1} + \frac{1}{f_2} - \frac{d}{f_1 f_2}$ and $P = P_1 + P_2 - dP_1P_2$.

7. **Focal length of a lens in different media:**

$$\frac{f_{liq}}{f_{air}} = \frac{{}^a\mu_g - 1}{\frac{{}^a\mu_g}{{}^a\mu_e} - 1}.$$

Where: ${}^a\mu_e$ = R. I. of liquid w.r.t. air, ${}^a\mu_g$ = R. I. of glass w.r.t. air.

8. **Newton's formula:** $\sqrt{u.v} = f$.

Where: u and v = object and image distance from principal focus.

9. **Formation of real image by a convex lens:** $D_{min} = 4f$.

10. **Focal length of a lens by displacement method:** $f = \frac{D^2 - d^2}{4D}$.

Where: D = distance between object and screen and d = displacement of lens.

11. **Lateral chromatic aberration** $= \frac{\omega}{f}$.

Where : ω = dispersive power and f = focal length.

12. **Achromatic lens:**

(*i*) single : $\frac{\omega}{f} = 0$.

(*ii*) Two lenses in contact : $\frac{\omega_1}{f_1} + \frac{\omega_2}{f_2} = 0$

or $\frac{\omega_1}{\omega_2} = -\frac{f_1}{f_2}$.

(*iii*) Two lenses separated by a distance d :

$$\frac{\omega_1}{f_1} + \frac{\omega_2}{f_2} - d\frac{\omega_1 + \omega_2}{f_1 f_2} = 0.$$

(*iv*) $d = \frac{1}{2}(f_1 + f_2)$ provided, $\omega_1 = \omega_2$.

13. Ratio of focal length of lens for violet and red rays : $\frac{f_v}{f_r} = \frac{\mu_r - 1}{\mu_v - 1}$.

14. **Hypermetropia or long sight :** $\frac{1}{f} = \frac{1}{D} - \frac{1}{d}$.

Where : f = focal length of correcting (convex) lens, d = near point of the faulty eye and D = near point of corrected eye.

15. **Myopia or short sight :** $\frac{1}{f} = \frac{1}{x} - \frac{1}{d}$. If $x = \infty$, $f = -d$. **Where:** d = far point of the faulty eye and x = far point of the corrected eye.

16. **Readymade formula :** $f = \frac{xy}{x-y}$.

Where : f = focal length of correcting lens, x = distance which can be clearly seen and y = distance which is to be seen.

(*i*) If $x > y$, f = +ve, convex lens (**Hypermetropia**).

(*ii*) If $x < y$, f = –ve, concave lens (**Myopia**).

Optical Instruments

1. **Simple microscope or magnifying glass:**

(*i*) $M = 1 + \frac{D}{f}$ (**for distinct setting**).

(*ii*) $M = 1 + \frac{D-a}{f}$

Where : a = distance of lens from eye.

(*iii*) $M' = \frac{D}{f}$ (for **normal setting**).

2. **Compound microscope** : For **distinct setting**:

$$M = M_o \times M_e = \frac{v_o}{u_o}\left(1 + \frac{D}{f_e}\right).$$

Where : M_o and M_e = magnification produced by objective lens and eye-piece respectively, u_o and v_o = object and image distance from the objective lens and f_e = focal length of eye-piece lens.

3. **Astronomical telescope :**

(*i*) For **normal setting** (image at ∞)

$$M = \frac{f_o}{f_e}.$$

(*ii*) $M = \frac{f_o}{f_e}\left(1 + \frac{f_e}{D}\right)$, for **distinct setting**.

(*iii*) The length (L) of telescope in all cases $= v_o + u_e$.

(*iv*) $L = f_o + f_e$ (for **normal setting**).

4. **Galilean telescope :**

(*i*) $M = \frac{f_o}{f_e}$ **(normal setting).**

(*ii*) $M = \frac{f_o}{f_e}\left(1 - \frac{f_e}{D}\right)$, **for distinct setting.**

(iii) Length $(L) = v_o - u_e = f_o - f_e$ **(normal setting)**

5. **Photographic camera :**

(*i*) $n = \frac{f}{d}$.

(*ii*) $\frac{t_1}{t_2} = \left(\frac{n_1}{n_2}\right)^2$.

Where : n = 'f' number, f = focal length, d = diameter of the stop and t_1 and t_2 are time of exposures.

Interference of Light

1. **For constructive interference :** Phase difference $(\delta) = 2n\pi$ and path difference $(\Delta) = n\lambda$.
Where : $n = 0$ or any integer.

2. For **destructive interference :**

$$\delta = (2n + 1)\pi \text{ and } \Delta = (2n+1)\frac{1}{2}\lambda.$$

3. $\delta = \frac{2\pi}{\lambda} \times \Delta.$

4. **Fring width** $(\beta) = \frac{\lambda D}{d}$; **(Young's double slit experiment).**

Where : d = distance between two coherent sources and

D = distance of the screen from the sources.

5. **Fresnel's biprism :**

(*i*) $\beta = \frac{\lambda D}{d}.$

(*ii*) $d = \sqrt{d_1 d_2}.$

Where : d_1 and d_2 = distance between the real images in two different position of the lens.

Doppler's Effect

1. $n' - n = \Delta n = \pm n\frac{v}{c}.$

Where : n = frequency when there is no relative motion, n' = apparent frequency, Δn = change in frequency, v = relative velocity between source and observer, c = velocity of light, +ve sign for approaching and –ve sign for receding.

2. $\Delta\lambda = \lambda' - \lambda = \pm\lambda\frac{v}{c}$.

Where : –ve sign for approaching and +ve sign for receding.

CHEMISTRY

1

ATOMIC STRUCTURE

1. Atomic Number (Z)
   = number of protons in the nucleus
   = number of electrons in neutral atom.
2. Mass Number (A)
   = no. of neutrons + no. of protons,
   i.e. $A = n + p$
3. Number of neutrons = $A - Z$.
4. Maximum no. of electrons in an orbit = $2n^2$
   Where: n = orbit no. or principal quantum number.
5. Maximum no. of electrons in a sub-shell
   $= 4n - 2 = 2(2l + 1) = 4l + 2$.
   Where: l = azimuthal quantum number.
6. For any value of n, there are n values of l and the value ranges from 0 to $n - 1$.
7. For any value of l, there are $2l + 1$ values of m and the value ranges from $-l$ to $+l$ including zero.
   Where: m = magnetic quantum number

8. For each value of n, there are n^2 values of m.
9. For a particular value of n, there are $2n^2$ sets of quantum numbers.
10. **Energy of electron in n^{th} orbit (E_n):**

(a) **In C.G.S. unit:**

$$E_n = -\frac{2\pi^2 m Z^2 e^4}{n^2 h^2} \text{ erg/electron.}$$

In another way, $E_n = -\frac{E_1}{n^2}$

Where: m = mass of electron = 9.11×10^{-28} gm; e = charge of an electron = -4.8×10^{-10} esu; Z = atomic number; h = Planck's constant = 6.625×10^{-27} erg.sec; E_n and E_1 represent the energies of electron in n^{th} and 1st orbits respectively.

(b) **In S.I. unit:**

$$E_n = -\frac{2\pi^2 m Z^2 e^4}{(4\pi \epsilon_0)^2 n^2 h^2} = -\frac{m Z^2 e^4}{8 \epsilon_0^2 n^2 h^2}$$

joule/electron.

Where: m = mass of electron = 9.11×10^{-31} kg; e = charge of an electron

$= 1.6 \times 10^{-19}$ coulomb; Z = atomic number; h = Planck's constant = 6.625×10^{-34} joule.sec; $4\pi\epsilon_0$ is called permitivity factor and is equal to

$$\frac{1}{9\times10^9} = \frac{(\text{Coulomb})^2}{\text{Newton}\times(\text{Metre})^2} = \frac{1}{9\times10^9}$$

$$= \frac{C^2}{N\times m^2};$$

ϵ_0 is called permitivity of free space

and is equal to $\frac{1}{36\pi\times10^9}\frac{C^2}{N\times m^2}$

$$= 8.854\times10^{-12}\ \frac{C^2}{N\times m^2}.$$

11. **Radius of the nth stationary orbit (r_n):**
   (a) **In C.G.S. unit:**

$$r_n = \frac{n^2h^2}{4\pi^2 mZe^2}$$ In another way,

$$r_n = \frac{n^2}{Z}\, r_o.$$

Where: r_n and r_o represent the radii of nth and 1st orbits respectively, r_o is called **first Bohr radius.**

N.B.: For hydrogen ($Z = 1$), $r_o = 0.529$ Å. Other notations have usual meaning.

(b) **In S.I. unit:**

$$r_n = \frac{(4\pi \epsilon_0)n^2h^2}{4\pi^2 mZe^2} = \frac{\epsilon_o n^2h^2}{\pi mZe^2}$$

Notations have usual meaning.

12. **Velocity of electron in n^{th} orbit (v_n):**

(a) **In C.G.S. unit:** $v_n = \dfrac{2\pi Ze^2}{nh}$ cm/sec.

In another way, $v_n = \dfrac{V_1}{n}$

Where: v_n and v_1 represent the velocities of electron in n^{th} and 1st orbits respectively.

(b) **In S.I. unit:** $v_n = \dfrac{Ze^2}{2 \epsilon_o nh}$ m/sec.

13. **Angular momentum of electron in n^{th} orbit:** $I\omega_n = mV_nR_n = \dfrac{nh}{2\pi}$

14. Radius of atom $\simeq 10^{-8}$ cm = 1 Angstrom unit (1 Å).
15. Radius of nucleus $\simeq 10^{-13}$ cm = 1 Fermi.
16. $E = h.v.$

    Where:

    E = energy;

    v = Frequency of radiation.

Isotopes

Atoms of same element are said to be isotopes of that element if they have same atomic number but different mass numbers or in other words, same number of protons and electrons but different neutron number.

such as $^{1}_{1}H$, $^{2}_{1}H$, $^{3}_{1}H$; $^{12}_{6}C$, $^{13}_{6}C$, $^{14}_{6}C$; $^{16}_{8}O$, $^{17}_{8}O$, $^{18}_{8}O$,

Isobars

Atoms of different elements are said to be isobars if they have same mass numbers though their atomic numbers are different. i.e., inspite of different number of neutrons and protons, the sum of $n + p$ is the same.

such as $^{40}_{18}Ar$, $^{40}_{19}K$, $^{40}_{20}Ca$.

Isotones

Atoms of different elements are said to be isotones if they have the same number of neutrons even though the atomic numbers and mass numbers are different.

Bohr's model of atom

Postulates of Bohr's theory

(*i*) The electrons revolve round the nucleus in closed circular orbits. Necessary centripetal forces for rotation is provided by the electrostatic force between the nucleus and the electon.

(*ii*) An electon can revolve only in certain discrete, non-radiating orbits, called stationary orbits. For these orbits, the total angular momentum of the moving electron is an integral multiple of $\frac{h}{2\pi}$.

(*iii*) The energy is radiated only when an electron jumps from one stationary orbit to another.

Atomic quantum numbers

1. **Principal quantum number (n):** The principal quantum number n corresponds to the principal energy level of the elctrons

It has integral positive values excluding zero.

2. **Angular quantum number or azimuthal quantum number (l):** Having the same principal level, there are different orbitals having different energy and different angular momentum. These orbitals are called *subshells* and are characterized by their orbital quantum number l, l can have all integral values from 0 to $(n - 1)$. If $l = 0$, 1, 2, 3 ... the sub-shells are called as *s, p, d, f* ..... respectively.

Shells	Values of n	Values of l	Representation of sub-shells
K	1	0	1s
L	2	0, 1	2s, 2p
M	3	0, 1, 2	3s, 3p, 3d
N	4	0, 1, 2, 3	4s, 4p, 4d, 4f

3. **Magnetic quantum number (m):** The changing the orientation of the electrons in space around the nucleus are determined by magnetic quantum numbers m. For a given value l, m can have any integral value from $-l$ to $+l$ including zero, i.e., for a given value of l, m can have of $(2l + 1)$ values.

Sub-Shells	Values of l	Values of m	Number of orbitals
s	0	0	1
p	1	−1, 0, +1	3
d	2	−2, −1, 0, +1, +2	5
f	3	−3, −2, −1, 0, +1, +2, +3	7

4. **Spin quantum number (s):** Spin quantum number determines the spining of an electron about its own axis and can have only two directions: clockwise or anti clockwise, can have either of the two values, $+\frac{1}{2}$ or $-\frac{1}{2}$.

2

RADIO ACTIVITY

1. $\frac{dN}{dt} = -\lambda N$

Where: $\frac{dN}{dt}$ is called rate of decay and λ is called decay constant or disintegration constant. –ve sign indicates that N decreases with lapse of time.

2. $T_A = \frac{1}{\lambda}$;

Where: T_A is mean life or average life.

3. $T_{1/2} = 0.693 \times T_A = 69.3\%$ of $T_{A;}$

Where: $T_{1/2}$ is half life.

4. $T_{1/2} = \frac{0.693}{\lambda} = \frac{\log e^2}{\lambda}$

5. $$\frac{N}{N_o} = \left(\frac{1}{2}\right)^n$$

Where: No = Original number or amount of nuclei; N = Number of undisintegrated nuclei after lapse of time t; n = Number of half lives passed and $n = \frac{t}{T_{1/2}}$.

6. $$\% \text{ Radioactivity} = \left(\frac{1}{2}\right)^n \times 100$$

7. **Remember:** Full life > Average life > Half life.

8. **Units of Radioactivity:**

   (a) **Curie:** It is the quantity of a radioactive substance which gives 3.7×10^{10} disintegrations/sec.

1 Curie = 3.7×10^{10} disintegrations/sec

1 Milli Curie (10^{-3} Curie) = 3.7×10^{7} disintegrations/sec

1 Micro Curie (10^{-6} Curie) = 3.7×10^{4} disintegrations/sec

(b) **Rutherford:** It is the quantity of a radioactive material which gives 10^6 disintegrations/sec.

1 Rutherford = 10^6 disintegrations/sec

1 Milli Rutherford = 10^3 disintegrations/sec

1 Micro Rutherford = 1 (one) disintegration/sec

(c) **Becquerel:** It is the quantity of a radioactive element which gives 1 (one) disintegration per second.

3

AVOGADRO'S LAW, MOLE CONCEPT, VAPOUR DENSITY AND MOLECULAR WEIGHT

1. 1 amu = 1.66×10^{-24} gm.

2. No. of moles $(n) = \dfrac{\text{wt. in gram}}{\text{Formula wt. (At. wt.; Mol. wt. or Ionic wt.)}}$

3. N (Avogadro's number) = 6.023×10^{23} particles (atoms, molecules, ions etc.).

4. 1 mole = mass of 6.023×10^{23} particles = 1 gm formula wt.

5. Wt. of a single particle (atom, molecule, ion etc.) = $\dfrac{\text{gram formula wt.}}{N}$

6. Molar volume of a gas = 22.4 litres at S.T.P or N.T.P.

7. Normal temperature = 0°C or 273°K and Normal pressure = 1 atmosphere or 760 mm of *Hg*.

8. Vapour Density $(V.D.) = \frac{W}{V} \times 11.2$

9. Molecular wt. $(M) = \frac{W}{V} \times 22.4$

   Where: V is the volume in litres at S.T.P. or N.T.P.

10. $M = 2 \times V.D.$

11. No. of moles after decomposition or dissociation = $1 + (n-1) \times \alpha$;

    Where: α is degree of dissociation, and

    n = no. of particles after dissociation.

12. $\frac{M_c}{M_o} = \frac{D_c}{D_o} = 1 + (n-1) \times \alpha$ in case of dissociation.

13. $\frac{M_c}{M_o} = \frac{D_c}{D_o} = 1 - \alpha\left(\frac{n-1}{n}\right)$ in case of association.

    Where: α = degree of association, c stands for calculated or normal value and o stands for observed or abnormal value.

4

EQUIVALENT WEIGHT AND ATOMIC WEIGHT

1. Equivalent weight of an element $= \dfrac{\text{At. wt.}}{\text{Valency}}$
2. 1 gram eq.wt. = eq.wt. in gram.
3. No. of gram equivalent

$$= \frac{\text{wt. in gram}}{\text{gram equivalent wt.}}$$

4. Equivalent wt. of an acid

$$= \frac{\text{Molecular wt.}}{\text{Basicity of an acid}}$$

5. Equivalent wt. of a base

$$= \frac{\text{Molecular wt.}}{\text{Acidity of a base}}$$

6. If no redox reaction, then equivalent wt. of a radical

$$= \frac{\text{Formula wt.}}{\text{Charge on ions (radicals) or valency}}$$

7. Eq. wt. of a compound

$$= \frac{\text{Molecular wt.}}{\text{Total charge of its cation or anion}}$$

= Sum of eq. wt. of elements and radicals

= Eq. wt. of cation + Eq. wt. of anion.

8. For reaction with $H_2 : E = \dfrac{w_1}{w_2(H)}$

$$= \frac{\text{wt. of metal}}{\text{wt. of } H_2} = \frac{w_1}{V} \times 11{,}200$$

9. For reaction with Chlorine :

$$E = \frac{w_1}{w_2(Cl)} \times 35.5 = \frac{w}{V} \times 11{,}200$$

$$= \frac{\text{wt. of element}}{\text{wt. of Chlorine}} \times 35.5$$

10. For reaction with Oxygen :

$$E = \frac{w_1}{w_2(O_2)} \times 8$$

$$= \frac{\text{wt. of substance}}{\text{wt. of Oxygen}} \times 8$$

$$= \frac{w_1}{V} \times 5{,}600$$

11. In general reaction : $\frac{w_1}{w_2} = \frac{E_1}{E_2}$

12. In redox reaction :
Equivalent wt. of a substance

$$= \frac{\text{Formula wt.}}{\text{No. of electrons lost or gained per molecule}}$$

$$= \frac{\text{Formula wt.}}{\text{Total change in oxidation number per molecule}}$$

13. For solid elements (except C, Si, B etc.) **(Dulong and Petit's law) :**
At. wt. × specific heat = 6.4 approx.
= Atomic heat.

14. $A = E \times x$ = Equivalent wt. × Valency.

15. $x = \dfrac{2 \times V.D.}{2(E+8)}$ in oxide and $x = \dfrac{2 \times V.D.}{E+35.5}$ in chloride.

16. For an isomorphous AX, BX,

$$= \frac{\text{wt. of } A \text{ that combines with } x \text{ gm of } X}{\text{wt. of } B \text{ that combines with } x \text{ gm of } X}$$

$$= \frac{\text{At. wt. of A}}{\text{At. wt. of B}}$$

5

GAS LAWS, GRAHM'S LAW AND DALTON'S LAW OF PARTIAL PRESSURE

For given mass of a gas:

1. $V \propto \frac{1}{P}$ *or* $PV = \text{const.}$

   or $P_1V_1 = P_2V_2$,

   T const. **Boyle's law.**

2. $V \propto T$ *or* $\frac{V}{T} = \text{const.}$

   or $\frac{V_1}{T_1} = \frac{V_2}{T_2}$,

   P const. : **Charles' law.**

3. $P \propto T$ or $\frac{P}{T} = const.$

or $\frac{P_1}{T_1} = \frac{P_2}{T_2}$,

V const. : **Gay Lussac's law**

4. (a) $t°\ C = (t + 273)°$ Abs. or $(t + 273)°$ K.
   (b) $t°C = T°\ K - 273$ = Abs. – 273
5. $V \propto n$, **Where:** P and T are const.

   (Avogadro's law)

   Thus, for the same P, V and T,
   $n_1 = n_2 = n_3 = \ldots\ldots\ldots\ldots$
6. Equation of state or ideal gas equation:
   (*i*) $PV = RT$ for 1 gm mole.
   (*ii*) $PV = nRT$ for n gm moles or

$$PV = \frac{m \text{ (mass)}}{M \text{ (mol. wt.)}} \times RT$$

Where: R = Gas const. = 0.0821 litres atm deg^{-1} mole^{-1}
= 8.31×10^7 ergs deg^{-1} mole^{-1}
= 8.31 joules deg^{-1} mole^{-1}
= 2 calories deg^{-1} mole^{-1}
= (1.987 calories exactly)

7. For the same mass of a gas : $\frac{P_1V_1}{T_1} = \frac{P_2V_2}{T_2}$

8. If mass changes, number of moles also changes.

In this case, $\frac{P_1V_1}{n_1T_1} = \frac{P_2V_2}{n_2T_2}$

9. $\frac{P_1}{d_1T_1} = \frac{P_2}{d_2T_2}$;

Where : d_1 and d_2 stand for densities.

10. Rate of diffusion or effusion $(r) = \frac{V(\text{volume})}{t(\text{time})}$

11. $\frac{r_1}{r_2} = \frac{\frac{V_1}{t_1}}{\frac{V_2}{t_2}} = \sqrt{\frac{D_2}{D_1}} = \sqrt{\frac{M_2}{M_1}}$

12. Partial pressure of a gas $(p) = \frac{nRT}{V}$

Where: V = Volume occupied by the mixture, T = temp. of the mixture and n = no. of moles of the gas.

13. Total pressure $(P) = p_1 + p_2 + p_3 + \dots\dots\dots + p_n$

$$= \Sigma n \frac{RT}{V}$$

Where: Σn is the total number of moles in the mixture.

14. $$\frac{\text{Partial pressure}}{\text{Total pressure}} = \frac{n}{\Sigma n} = \text{mole fraction.}$$

15. $$P = \frac{P_1V_1 + P_2V_2 + P_3V_3 + \dots\dots}{\text{Total volume}}$$

6

KINETIC THEORY OF GASES

Symbols used:

P = pressure of gas.
C = R.M.S velocity.
α = most probable speed.
m = mass of each molecule of the gas.
n = no. of molecules of the gas.
M = mol. wt.
T = absolute temp.
λ = mean free path.
ρ = density of the gas.
K = Boltzman's const. = $\frac{R}{N}$ [N = Avogadro's no.]
v_{av} = mean or average vel.
V = volume of one mole of the gas
R = gas const.
d = diameter of each molecule.
η = co-efficient of viscosity.

1. $v_{av} = 0.9213 \times C.$
2. $\alpha = 0.816 \times C.$
3. $PV = \frac{1}{3} mnC^2 = \frac{1}{3} MC^2$
4. $C = \sqrt{\frac{3PV}{M}} = \sqrt{\frac{3P}{\rho}} = \sqrt{\frac{3RT}{M}} = \sqrt{\frac{3KT}{m}}$
5. $v_{av} = \frac{v_1 + v_2 + ... + v_n}{n} = \sqrt{\frac{8RT}{\pi M}} = \sqrt{\frac{8KT}{\pi m}}$
6. $C = \sqrt{\frac{C_1^2 + C_2^2 + ... + Cn^2}{n}}$
7. $\alpha = \sqrt{\frac{2RT}{M}} = \sqrt{\frac{2KT}{m}}$
8. Translatory kinetic energy/mole $= \frac{3}{2} RT$

$$= \frac{1}{2} MC^2$$

9. $\lambda = \eta \sqrt{\frac{3}{P\rho}} \simeq \frac{m}{\pi d^2 \rho} = \frac{m}{\sqrt{2} \pi d^2 \rho}$

7

EUDIOMETRY OR GAS ANALYSIS

1. One mole of all gases occupy 22.4 litres at S.T.P.
2. Equal no. of moles occupy equal volume at the same temperature and pressure.
3. Volume of solid or liquid is considered negligible in comparision to the volume of a gas.
4. For the determination of formula of a hydrocarbon :

$$C_xH_y + (x + \frac{1}{4}y)O_2 = xCO_2 + \frac{1}{2}yH_2O$$

5. For one c c of hydrocarbon :

   (a) Volume of CO_2 produced = x c c

   (b) Volume of O_2 required = $x + \frac{1}{4}y$ c c

(c) Contraction in volume = $1+\frac{1}{4}ycc$

6.

Absorbant	Gas absorbed
NaOH or KOH soln.	CO_2, SO_2, Halogens, NO_2
Ammonical cuprous chloride	CO, C_2H_2
Turpentine	O_3
$FeSO_4$ soln.	NO
Alkaline Pyragallol	O_2
Heated Palladium	H_2
Heated Magnesium	N_2
Conc. H_2SO_4	moisture, NH_3

8

TITRATION

1. Normality $(N) = \frac{w}{V} \times \frac{1000}{E}$

   Where: V in ml.

2. $N = \frac{\text{gm. litre}^{-1}}{\text{Eq. wt.}}$

   $= \frac{\text{wt. of solute in gm/litre soln.}}{\text{eq. wt. of solute}}$

3. Molarity $(M) = \frac{\text{gram. litre}^{-1}}{\text{Molecular wt.}}$

4. $M = \frac{w}{V} \times \frac{1000}{\text{Mol. wt.}}$

   Where: V in ml.

5. $V_1S_1 + V_2S_2 + V_3S_3 + \ldots\ldots\ldots = V_m \times S_m$,

   For mixture containing all acids or alkalies.

6. $\{V_1S_1$ (acid one) + V_2S_2 (acid two) + ...$\}$ – $\{V'S'$ (alkali one) + V'' S'' (alkali two)+ ....$\}$ = V_mS_m; For mixture containing acids and alkalies.

7. $$\text{Factor} = \frac{\text{wt. of the solute taken}}{\text{wt. of the solute required for desired strength}}$$

8. Actual strength = Factor × Approximate strength.

N.B.:

(a) For mono-basic acid (HCl) or mono-acidic base (KOH); Molarity (M) = Normality (N); [∵ Mol. wt. = Eq. wt.]

(b) For di-basic acid (H_2SO_4) or di-acidic base [$Ca(OH)_2$]; $M = 2(N)$; [∵ Mol. wt. = 2 × Eq. wt.]

(c) For tri-basic acid H_3PO_4 or tri-acidic base [$Al(OH)_3$]; M = 3(N); [∵ Mol. wt. = 3 × Eq. wt.]

9

ELECTRO CHEMISTRY

Electrode Potential, E.M.F. and Electrolysis

1. Equivalent conductance, $\Lambda = \dfrac{\sigma \times 1000}{C}$
2. Molar conductance, $\Lambda_m = \dfrac{\sigma \times 1000}{M}$
3. According to Kohlrausch's law,

$$\Lambda_m^{\infty} = n_+ \Lambda_{m+}^{\infty} + n_- \Lambda_{m-}^{\infty}$$

4. $$E\left(M^{+n}/M\right) = E^\circ\left(M^{n+}/M\right) - \frac{2.303\,RT}{nF}$$

$$\log \frac{[M(s)]}{\left[M^{n+}(aq)\right]}$$ (Nerns't equation)

5. $E^\circ_{cell} = 2.303\,\dfrac{RT}{nF}\log K_c$

6. $\Delta G° = -nFE°_{cell} = -2.303 RT \log K_c$
7. $m = WIt$ (Faraday's law of electrolysis)

Conductors and insulators

The substances which permit the passage of electric current through them, are called as conductors. But the substances which do not permit the passage of electric current through them, are called as non-conductors or insulators. Metals are good conductors of electricity.

Electrolytes and non-electrolytes

The substances which permit the passage of electric current through their molten state or in solution and are decomposed by it, are known as **electrolytes**. This phenomenon of passage of electric current through an electrolytic solution is known as **electrolytic conduction**. While, the substances which do not permit the passage of electric current through their molten state or in solution and are not decomposed by it, are known as **non-electrolytes**.

I. **Specific resistance or resistivity:** Specific resistance or resistivity of the material of a conductor is defined as the resistance of unit length and unit area of cross-section of that conductor.

Now specific resistance or resistivity is given as,

$$\rho = R\frac{A}{l}$$

Whare R = Resistance of the conductor

A = Area of cross-section of the conductor

l = Length of the conductor.

Its SI unit is ohm metre (Ω m).

II. Conductance: The reciprocal of the resistance of a conductor is called its conductance. It is denoted by G.

So,

$$G = \frac{1}{R}$$

Its SI unit is mho or ohm^{-1} (Ω^{-1}).

III. Specific conductance or conductivity: The reciprocal of the resistivity of the material of a conductor is called its conductivity. It is denoted by σ. Hence,

$$\sigma = \frac{1}{\rho}$$

Its SI unit is ohm^{-1} metre^{-1} ($\Omega^{-1}\ m^{-1}$).

IV. **Equivalent conductance:** Equivalent conductance is defined as the conductance of a volume of solution containing one gram equivalent of an electrolyte in solution. It is denoted by symbol Λ. Its unit is ohm^{-1} cm^2 $(g\text{-}equiv)^{-1}$.

Now, $$\Lambda = \frac{\sigma \times 1000}{C}$$

Where σ = specific conductance.

C = equivalents of solute per litre of solution.

V. **Molar conductance** is defined as the conductance of a volume of solution containing one gram mole of an electrolyte in solution. It is denoted by Λ_m. Its unit is ohm^{-1} cm^2 mol^{-1}.

Now, $$\Lambda_m = \frac{\sigma \times 1000}{M}$$

Where σ = specific conductance.

M = concentration of the solution in moles per litre.

VI. **Electrolytic cell:** It is a device used to convert electrical energy into chemical energy. Reduction takes place at cathode and oxidation takes placed at anode. When electricity is passed through electrolyte, it dissociates into its ions, cations move towards the cathode and anions move towards the anode. When electricity is passed through molten sodium chloride, then,

Electrochemical reaction, $NaCl \rightleftharpoons Na^+ + Cl^-$

At cathode : $Na^+ + e^- \rightarrow Na$ (reduction)

At anode : $Cl^- - e^- \rightarrow Cl$ (oxidation)

$Cl + Cl \rightarrow Cl_2$

VII. **Faraday's laws of electrolysis:**

First law of electrolysis: During electrolysis, the mass of the substance produced or consumed at an electrode is directly proportional to the quantity of electricity passed through the electrolyte.

Hence, $m = WIt$

Second law of electrolysis: When the same quantity of electricity is passed through different electrolytes connected in series, the weight of different substances produced at the electrodes are proportional to their equivalent weight.

VIII. **Commercial cell or batteries:** A battery is a series combination of two or more electrochemical cells used as a source of electrical energy. Following are the types of commercial cells.

Commercial cell

Primary cells	Secondary cells or storage cells or accumulators
(They cannot be recharged) e.g. dry cell, mercury cell.	(They can be reacharged) e.g. lead storage cell, nickel cadmium cell, fuel cells.

IX. **Electrolytic corrosion:** Corrosion is the gradual deterioration of metal by atmospheric attack. It is an electrochemical reaction. Corrosion of iron is called as rusting. Rust is mainly a mixture of ferric hydroxide $[Fe(OH)_3]$ and ferric oxide $[Fe_2O_3.]$.

Factors Affecting Molar Conductance

(a) **Nature of electrolytes:** If greater the number of ions in the solution, then greater is the conductance. Strong electrolytes dissociate completely into its ions and give large number of ions, therefore have high conductance. Weak electrolytes ionize to small extent and give lesser number of ions, so have low conductance.

(b) Concentration of the solution: Molar conductance of an elctrolyte increases with decrease in concentration.

For strong electrolytes, variation of molar conductance with concentration is given as,

$$\Lambda_m = \Lambda_m^{\infty} - b\sqrt{C}$$

Where Λ_m^{∞} = molar conductance at infinite dilution

C = concentration

b = a constant

(c) Temperature: The conductance of electrolytes increases with increase in temperature.

Kohlrausch's Law of Independant Migration of Ions

According to this law *at infinite dilution, if dissociation for all electrolytes is complete and if all inter-ionic effects disappear each ion migrates independently, and contributes to the total equivalent conductance of an electrolyte a definite share which depends only on its own nature and not at all on that of the ion with which it is associated.* So,

Λ_m of any electrolyte is the sum of the molar conductances of the ions composing it. Molar conductances of cations and anions at infinite dilution are represented as

Λ^{∞}_{m+} and Λ^{∞}_{m-} respectively. Now,

$$\Lambda^{\infty}_{m} = n_+ \Lambda^{\infty}_{m+} + n_- \Lambda^{\infty}_{m-}$$

where n_+ and n_- are the number of cations and anions per formula unit of electrolyte.

For NaCl, $\Lambda^{\infty}_{m}(\text{NaCl}) = \Lambda^{\infty}_{m+}\left(\text{Na}^+\right) + \Lambda^{\infty}_{m-}\left(\text{Cl}^-\right)$.

For $Al_2(SO_4)_3$, $\Lambda^{\infty}_{m}\left[Al_2(SO_4)_3\right] = 2\Lambda^{\infty}_{m+}\left(Al^{3+}\right)$

$+ 3\Lambda^{\infty}_{m-}\left(SO_4^{2-}\right)$

Differences Between Electrochemical Cell and Electrolytic Cell

Electrochemical Cell (or galvanic cell or valtaic cell)	Electrolytic cell
I. It is a device used to convert chemical energy into electrical energy	I. It is a device used to convert electrical energy into chemical energy.

II. Cell reaction is spontaneous.	II. Cell reaction is non-spontaneous.
III. Free energy decreases as the cell reaction proceeds.	III. Free energy increases as the cell reaction proceeds.
IV. Work is obtained from the cell.	IV. Work is done on the cell.
V. The two electrodes are placed in different containers called *half cells*, connected through *salt bridge*.	V. Both the electrodes are placed in the same container.
VI. Oxidation occurs at anode (negative terminal) and reduction occurs at cathode (positive terminal).	VI. Oxidation occurs at cathode (negative) and reduction occurs at anode (positive).

Electrochemical Cell

In electrochemical cell, electricity is produced by spontaneous chemical reaction. In redox-reaction simultaneous loss and gain of electrons takes place. The electrons lost by reducing agents are taken up by oxidising agent, which causes the transfer of electrons and produced electricity. Electrochemical cells are also called as voltaic cells or galvanic cells.

Voltaic cell consists of zinc rod dipped in 1.0M copper sulphate solution. Electrons pass from zinc atoms to copper ions in which they are in direct contact with each other.

Oxidation half reaction:

$$Zn\ (s) \rightarrow Zn^{2+}\ (aq) + 2e^-$$

Reduction half reaction:

$$Cu^{2+}(aq) + 2e^- \rightarrow Cu(s)$$

Overall reaction:

$$Zn(s) + Cu^{2+}(aq) \rightarrow Zn^{2+}(aq) + Cu(s)$$

Zinc Cupric ion Zinc ion Copper

Hence, It is represented as Zn (s) | Zn^{2+} (1M) || Cu^{2+} (1M) | Cu (s).

Daniel cell: It consists of two half cells, anode half cell and cathode half cell. The anode half cell consists of zinc electrode (anode) immersed in zinc sulphate solution and cathode half cell consists of copper electrode (cathode) immersed in copper sulphate solution. These two electrodes are connected with a copper wire through ammeter. The two solutions are connected through salt bridge.

At anode:

$$Zn(s) \rightarrow Zn^{2+}\ (aq) + 2e^- \quad \text{(oxidation)}$$

At cathode:

$$Cu^{2+}\ (aq) + 2e^- \rightarrow Cu\ (s) \qquad \text{(reduction)}$$

Electrochemical reaction:

$$Zn(s) + Cu^{2+}(aq) \rightarrow Zn^{2+}(aq) + Cu(s).$$

As the reaction starts, the mass of zinc rod decreases and that of copper rod increases.

Salt bridge: Salt bridge contains an inert paste of a strong electrolyte (Na_2SO_4 or KCl) and agar gel. Which prevents the mixing of two electrolytes and allows the migration of ions from cathode half cell to anode half cell.

Electrode Potential and E.M.F. of a Cell

Electrode potential: Electrode potenital is defined as the tendency of a metal to lose or gain electrons when placed in contact with its ions. It is of two types :

(a) **Oxidation potential:** The tendency of an electrode to lose electrons is known as its oxidation potential.

$Zn \rightleftharpoons Zn^{2+}(aq) + 2e^-$

(b) **Reduction potential:** The tendency of an electrode to gain electrons is known as its reduction potential.

$Cu^{2+}(aq) + 2e^- \rightleftharpoons Cu$

Oxidation potential is equal and opposite of reduction potential.

The electrode potential depends upon

(*a*) Concentration of metal ions in solution.

(*b*) Nature of the metal and its ions.

(*c*) Temperature.

E.M.F. or Cell Potential

The difference between the electrode potentials of the two electrodes providing an electrochemical cell is called, as electromotive force (E.M.F.) or cell potenital of a cell. Which is represented as E_{cell} and expressed in volts.

$$E_{cell} = E_{cathode} - E_{anode}$$

Distinctions Between E.M.F. and Potential Difference

E.M.F	Potential difference
I. It is the potential difference between the two electrodes when no current is being drawn from the cell i.e., in open circuit.	I. It is the difference of potentials of two electrodes when current is being drawn from the cell i.e., in closed circuit.
II. It is measured with the help of a potentiometer.	II. It is measured with the help of a voltmeter.

III. It is the maximum voltage that can be drawn from the cell.	III. It is less than the E.M.F. of the cell.
IV. It is a measure of maximum useful work obtainable from the cell.	IV. It gives work which is less than the maximum obtainable work.

1. $M^{n+} + ne = M$
2. $E_{Ox} + E_{Red}$ = e.m.f (of cell) in Volt.
3. $\Delta G = -nEF$;

   Where: ΔG = Change in free energy, n = no. of electrons used in the reaction, E = e.m.f. of cell and F = Faraday's constant = 96,500 coulombs
4. $\log K_e = \dfrac{nEF}{2.303\,RT}$ At 25°C, T = 273 + 25

   = 298 K and $\dfrac{2.303}{F} = 0.059$ so, at 25°C

   $$\log K_e = \frac{nE}{0.059}$$

   Where: K_e = equilibrium constant, E = e.m.f of cell and n = no. of electrons used in the reaction.
5. **Nernst equation:** For :

   $$M_1^{n+} + M_2 \rightleftharpoons M_1 + M_2^{n+}$$

$$E_{ox} = E^o{}_{ox} - \frac{2.303\ RT}{nF} \log K_e;$$

Where: E_{ox} = Oxidation potential and $E^o{}_{ox}$ = Standard oxidation potential

6. $w = ZQ = Z.i.t$ (1st law of electrolysis)

7. $Z = \frac{E}{F} \therefore w = \frac{E}{F}$.

8. $1\,F = 96{,}500$ coulombs $= N \times e = 6.023 \times 10^{23} \times 1.6 \times 10^{-19}$ coulombs.

9. $\frac{w_A}{w_B} = \frac{E_A}{E_B}$ (2nd law of electrolysis)

10. $\frac{Z_A}{Z_B} = \frac{E_A}{E_B}$;

Where: Z is called electrochemical equivalent and E is called chemical equivalent of the substance.

11. Oxidation occurs at anode.
12. Reduction occurs at cathode.
13. $1F \equiv 1$ gram equivalent of a substance $= 11{,}200$ ml H_2 at N.T.P. $= 5{,}600$ ml O_2 at N.T.P.
14. Unit of Z is the unit of mass per unit charge.

THEORY OF DILUTE SOLUTIONS

I. Mole percent of a component

$$= \frac{\text{Number of moles of that component}}{\text{Total number of moles in solution}} \times 100$$

II. Molarity of the solution

$$= \frac{\text{Number of moles of the solute}}{\text{Volume of the solution in litres}}$$

III. Molality of the solution

$$= \frac{\text{Number of moles of the solute}}{\text{Mass of the solvent in kg}}$$

IV. Formality of the solution

$$= \frac{\text{Number of formula masses of the solute}}{\text{Volume of the solution in litres}}$$

V. Normality of the solution

$$= \frac{\text{Number of gram equivalents of the solute}}{\text{Volume of the solution in litres}}$$

VI. Normality = Molarity × $\frac{\text{Molar mass}}{\text{Equivalent mass}}$

VII. Normality (for acids) = Molarity × Basicity

VIII. Normality (for bases) = Molarity × Acidity

Solution, Solute and Solvent

A solution is a homogeneous mixture of two or more substances. A solution of two substances is called a binary solution. Its two components are called as solute and solvent.

A substance which is dissolved into another substance is called as **solute** and another substance which dissolves the solute into it is called as solvent. In sugar solution sugar is solute and water is **solvent**.

Types of Solutions

S.No.	Physical state of Solute	Solvent	Solution	Examples
I	Solid	Solid	Solid	Alloys geme etc
II	Liquid	Solid	Solid	Mercury in zinc or gold (amalgams) etc.

III.	Gas	Solid	Solid	Hydrogen in palladium etc.
IV.	Solid	Liquid	Liquid	Sugar in water, salt in wate etc.
V.	Liquid	Liquid	Liquid	Alcohol in water, benzene in toluene etc.
VI.	Gas	Liquid	Liquid	Oxygen in water, CO_2 in water etc.
VII.	Solid	Gas	Gas	Dust particles in air, iodine in air etc.
VIII.	Liquid	Gas	Gas	Water in air (like humidity) etc.
IX.	Gas	Gas	Gas	Mixture of various gases, air etc.

Solubility

The maximum amout of any solute that can be dissolved in 100 g of solvent at a particular temperature is called the solubility of that solute at particulare temperature. Which depends upon

(*i*) nature of solute

(*ii*) nature of solvent

(*iii*) temperature of the solution

(*iv*) pressure (for gases)

1. Normality (N) = $\frac{w}{W} \times \frac{1000}{E}$; where, V in ml.

2. $N = \dfrac{\text{gm. litre}^{-1}}{\text{Eq. wt}}$

$$= \frac{\text{wt. of solute in gm./litre soln.}}{\text{Eq. wt. of solute}}$$

3. Molarity (M) = $\dfrac{\text{gram. litre}^{-1}}{\text{Molecular wt.}}$

4. $M = \dfrac{w}{V} \times \dfrac{1000}{\text{Mol. wt.}}$; where, V in ml.

5. $V_1S_1 + V_2S_2 + V_3S_3 + ... = V_m \times S_m$.
   For mixture containing all acids or alkalies.

6. $\{V_1S_1$ (acid one) + V_2S_2 (acid two) + ...} – V′S′(alkali one) + V″S″(alkali two) + ...
   = V_mS_m; For mixture containing acids and alkalies.

7. Factor

$$= \frac{\text{wt. of the solute taken}}{\text{wt. of the solute required for desired strength}}$$

8. Actual Strength = Factor × Approximate Strength.

N.B.

(*a*) For mono-basic acid (HCl) or mono-acidic base (KOH); Molarity (M) = Normality (N);
[∵ Mol. wt. = Eq.wt.]

(*b*) For di-basic acid (H_2SO_4) or di-acidic base [$Ca(OH)_2$];
M = 2(N); [∵ Mol. wt. = 2 × Eq. wt.]

(*c*) For tri-basic acid (H_3SO_4) or tri-acidic base [$Al(OH)_3$]; M = 3(N);
[∵ Mol. wt. = 3 × Eq. wt.]

OSMOTIC PRESSURE (P) :

1. $$P = \frac{nRT}{V} = \frac{m}{M} \times \frac{RT}{V} = CRT$$

Where: n = no. of moles of solute, T = temperature in °K, V = Volume in litres containing x gm mole of solute, C = Molar concentration of a solution, R is called solution constant and is analogous to gas constant.

2. $PV = RT$;
Where: V = vol. in litre containing 1 gm mole.

3. $$\frac{P_1V_1}{n_1T_1} = \frac{P_2V_2}{n_2T_2}$$ (in case of two solutions)

4. For two isotonic solutions at the same temperature , $\frac{V_1}{n_1} = \frac{V_2}{n_2}$

5. For two isotonic solutions, if $V_1 = V_2$, then $n_1 = n_2$ at the same temperature.

6. In case of dissociation:

$$\frac{M_c}{M_o} = \frac{P_o}{P_c} = 1 + (n-1)\alpha$$

Where: α is degree of dissociation.

7. In case of association of molecules,

$$\frac{M_c}{M_o} = \frac{P_o}{P_c} = \left(\frac{n-1}{n}\right)\alpha$$

Where: *o* stands for observed or abnormal value and *c* stands for theoretical or calculated or normal value.

8. In case of dissociation : Actual concentration $= \{1 + (n-1)\alpha\}\, C$ and $P_c = \{1 + (n-1)\alpha\}\, CRT$.

LOWERING OF VAPOUR PRESSURE (ΔP):

1. Lowering of Vapour Pressure $(\Delta P) = P - P_s$ **Where:** P = V.P. of pure solvent and P_s = V.P. of solution.

2. $\frac{\Delta P}{P} = \frac{P - P_s}{P} = \frac{n}{n+N}$;

$[\frac{n}{n+N}$ = mole fraction of the solute]

3. $\frac{\Delta P}{P} = \frac{P - P_s}{P} = \frac{m}{w} \times \frac{W}{M}$

Where: M = Mol. wt. of solute, W = Mol. wt. of solvent, m = wt. of solute in gm and w = wt. of solvent in gm.

$\frac{\Delta P}{P} = \frac{P - P_s}{P}$ = Relative lowering of $V.P.$

ELEVATION IN BOILING POINT (B.P.) (ΔT_b):

1. ΔT_b = B.P. of solution – B.P. of pure solvent.
2. $\Delta T_b \simeq C_m$ **(Raoult's law)**;
   Where: C_m is the molal or molar concentration of solution.
3. $\Delta T_b = \frac{K_b \times 10^3 \times w}{W \times M}$;

   Where: w = mass of solute in gm, W = mass of solvent in gm, M = Mol.wt. of solute and K_b = molal elevation constant of a solute.

4. $K_b = \frac{RT^2}{10^3 \times L} = \frac{0.002T^2}{L}$;

Where: L = Latent heat, T = b.p. and $R = 2$ cals deg^{-1} mole^{-1}.

5. $M = \frac{K_b \times 10^3 \times w}{\Delta T_b \times W}$

DEPRESSION IN FREEZING POINT (ΔT_f):

1. ΔT_f = F.P. of pure solvent – F.P. of solution.

2. $\Delta T_f = \frac{K_f \times 10^3 \times w}{W \times M}$

3. $K_f = \frac{0.002T^2}{L}$

Where: K_f is molal depression const. of a solvent and T is F.P.

4. Mol. wt. (M) = $\frac{K_f \times 10^3 \times w}{W \times \Delta T_f}$

5. For same solution $\frac{\Delta T_b}{\Delta T_f} = \frac{K_b}{K_f}$

N.B.: Rest symbols have usual meaning as mentioned in elevation in B.P.

11

THERMO CHEMISTRY

Some Basic Definitions

1. **Exothermic reaction:** The reaction in which heat is evolved, is called exothermic reaction.
2. **Endothermic reaction:** The reaction in which heat is absorbed, is called endothermic reaction.
3. **System:** It is that specified space of the universe which is under theromodynamic observation. It may be homogeneous or heterogeneous.
4. **Surroundings:** The remaining part of the universe that is outside the sytem, is called its surrounding. They are separated from each other by a real or imaginary boundary.
5. **State variables or state functions:** It is a measurable physical property of the system whose value depends only upon the state of

the sytem and not upon the path followed to attain this state. Some common state functions are: pressure (P), volume (V), temperature (T), internal energy (E), entropy (S), enthalpy (H) and free energy (G). Out of these function, **two state functions are sufficient to describe the state of any thermodynamic system.**

6. **Isothermal process:** A process during which the temperature of the system remains constant, is known as isothermal process.
7. **Adiabatic process:** A process during which the total quantity of heat of the sytem remains constant i.e., the heat is not allowed to enter or leave the system, is known as adiabatic process.
8. **Isochoric process:** A process during which the volume of the system remains constant, is known as isochoric process.
9. **Isobaric process:** A process during which the pressure of the system remains constant, is known as isobaric process.
10. **Irreversible process:** A process in which the direction of the process can not be reversed, is known as irreversible process.

11. **Reversible process:** A process in which direction of the process can be reversed by an infinitesimally small change in the state of the system, is known as reversible process.
12. **Cyclic process:** A process in which a system after undergoing a number of changes returns back to its original state, is known as cyclic process.

First Law of Thermodynamics

It states that, energy can neither be created nor destroyed but can be transformed from one form to another form. The total energy of an isolated system remains constant. Mathematically,

$$\Delta E = Q + W \quad \text{...}(i)$$

Where ΔE = change in internal energy

Q = heat given to the system

W = work done on the system

But $W = -P.\Delta V$

So, $\Delta E = Q - P.\Delta V \quad \text{...}(ii)$

$\Rightarrow \quad Q = \Delta E + P.\Delta V$

At constant volume, $\Delta V = 0$. So, $Q = \Delta E$

Hence, at constant volume, internal energy change is equal to heat of the system.

Enthaply (H) and Enthalpy Change (ΔH)

It is defined as the sum of internal energy and pressure-volume work of the system. So,

$$H = E + PV \qquad ...(i)$$

Like internal energy, enthalpy is also a state function. Its absolute value cannot be measured hence it is measured as change between two states A and B of the process.

$$\Delta H = H_B - H_A$$

From eq. (*i*) $\Delta H = \Delta E + P.\Delta V + V.\Delta P$

$$= Q + V\,\Delta P$$

At constant pressure, $\Delta P = 0$. Hence $\Delta H = Q$

Hence, **at constant pressure, enthalpy change is equal to heat of the sytem.**

For an exothermic reaction, $\Delta H = -ve$

For an endothermic reaction, $\Delta H = +ve$

Its SI unit is J mol^{-1} or kJ mol^{-1}.

Characteristics of Enthalpy

(*i*) Enthalpy is a state function.

(*ii*) Enthalpy change is independent of the path followed.

(*iii*) Enthalpy is an extensive property and its value depends upon the amount of substace.

Entropy (S)

Entropy is a measure of the degree of disorder of a system. Disorder of a system is measured by the energy absorbed by the system to attain that disorder. Gaseous state is the most disordered and therfore has the highest entropy.

For a reversible process at constant temperature, the change in entropy is,

$$\Delta s = \frac{Q}{T}$$

where Q = heat absorbed or evolved

T = constant temperature

If heat is absorbed in the process, $\Delta s = +$ ve

If heat is evolved in the process, $\Delta s = -$ve.

SI unit of entropy is JK^{-1}.

Second aw of Thermodynamics

It states that the change in entropy for every spontaneous process must always be positive and hence the entropy of universe always increases.

Characteristic of Entropy

(*i*) Entropy is a state function. Hence entropy change

$$\Delta S = S_{\text{final state}} - S_{\text{initial state}}$$

(ii) Entropy change is independent of the path followed.

(iii) Entropy is an extensive property and its value depends upon the amount of substance.

(iv) Entropy of the universe alwasy increases.

(v) Entropy change for a cyclic process is zero.

(vi) Entropy change for a reversible process is zero.

(vii) Entropy change for an irreversible spontaneous process is always greater than zero. i.e. $\Delta S > 0$.

Free Energy (G)

Gibb's free energy or simply free energy (G) is defined as the maximum available energy of the system which can be converted into useful work.

$$G = H - TS$$

where, H = enthalpy of the system

S = entropy of the system

T = absolute temperature of the system

At constant temperature, free energy change is given by,

$$\Delta G = \Delta H - T\Delta S$$

This is called is **Gibbs Helmholtz equation.**

Criterion for Feasibility of a Chemical Process

Only those chemical process are feasible or spontaneous in which free energy decreases i.e. ΔG is negative. There are three possibilities for ΔG:

(*i*) **ΔG is Zero.** In this case, the process does not proceed in any direction and is said to be in **equilibrium state.**

(*ii*) **ΔG is positive.** In this case, the reaction is non-spontaneous.

(*iii*) **ΔG is negative.** In this case, the reaction is spontaneous.

Conditions for Spontaneous Processes (i.e. ΔG to be negative)

The conditions for spontaneous processes and the effect of temperature.

$$(\Delta G = \Delta H - T\,\Delta S)$$

	Sign of		**Temperature**	**Nature of process**
ΔH	**$T\Delta S$**	**ΔG**	**(T)**	
–ve (i.e. exothermic)	+ve	–ve		Spontaneous

–ve (i.e. exothermic)	–ve	–ve	Low ($T\,\Delta S < \Delta H$)	Spontaneous
		+ve	High ($T\,\Delta S > \Delta H$)	Non-Spontaneous
+ve (i.e. endothermic)	–ve	+ve		Non-Spontaneous
+ve (i.e. endothermic)	+ve	+ve	Low ($T\,\Delta S < \Delta H$)	Non-Spontaneous
		–ve	High ($T\,\Delta S > \Delta H$)	Spontaneous
Zero	+ve	–ve		Spontaneous
Zero	–ve	+ve		Non-Spontaneous

So, a process or reaction takes place in such a way that free energy is minimum.

Characteristics of free energy

(*i*) Free energy is a state function. Hence free energy change
$\Delta G = G_{\text{final state}} - G_{\text{initial state}}$

(*ii*) Free energy change is independent of the path followed.

(*iii*) Free energy is an extensive property and its value depends upon the amount of substance.

(*iv*) $\Delta G_{\text{system}} = T\Delta S_{\text{universe}}$

(*v*) Free energy change gives the maximum useful work obtained from a process.

(*vi*) Free energy always decreases (or free energy change is always negative) during a spontaneous process.

Third law of thermodynamics

It states that, at absolute zero, the entropy of a perfectly crystalline substance may be taken as zero.

Standard entropy change ($\Delta S°$)

The entropy of one mole of substance at 298 K and 1 atm pressure is called as standard entropy ($S°$)

Standard entropy change in a reaction

= (sum of standard entropies of products)

– (sum of standard entropies of reactants)

or $\Delta S° = \Sigma S°$ (products) – $\Sigma S°$ (reactants)

Limitations of thermodynamics

(*i*) It deals with microscopic systems and does not tell anything about macroscopic system.

(*ii*) It deals with only initial and final states of the sytem.

1. Intrinsic energy = – Heat of formation
= **Enthalpy change of formation.**
2. For exothermic reaction:
$\Delta H = H_P - H_R = -Q$, i.e. $H_P < H_R$.
3. For endothermic reaction:
$\Delta H = H_P - H_R = +Q$, i.e. $H_P > H_R$.
4. ΔH_V be heat of reaction at const. vol. and ΔH_P be heat of reaction at const. pressure, then :
$\Delta H_P = \Delta H_V + \Delta nRT$;
Where: Δn = change in no. of moles = no. of moles of gaseous products – no. of moles of gaseous reactants.
If $\Delta n > 0$, then $\Delta H_P > \Delta H_V$.
If $\Delta n < 0$, then $\Delta H_P < \Delta H_V$.
If $\Delta n = 0$, then $\Delta H_V = \Delta H_P$.
5. **Kirchoff's equation:**
$\Delta H_P = \Delta C_P (T_2 - T_1)$

12

LAW OF MASS ACTION

1. For a reversible reaction:

$$A + B \rightleftharpoons C + D, K_C = \frac{[C][D]}{[A][B]}$$

2. For a general reversible reaction :

$$aA + bB \rightleftharpoons cC + dD$$

$$K_C = \frac{[C]^c[D]^d}{[A]^a[B]^b} \text{ and } K_P = \frac{P_C{}^c \times P_D{}^d}{P_A{}^a \times P_B{}^b}$$

3. $K_P = K_C (RT)^{\Delta n}$;

Where: Δn = change in no. of moles = No. of moles of products – no. of moles of reactants.

If $\Delta n > 0$, $K_P > K_C$. [$PCl_5 \rightleftharpoons PCl_3 + Cl_2$]

If $\Delta n < 0$, $K_P < K_C$. [$N_2 + 3H_2 \rightleftharpoons 2NH_3$]

If $\Delta n = 0$, $K_P = K_C$. [$2HI \rightleftharpoons H_2 + I_2$]

Where: K_C = Concentration equilibrium const. and K_P = Partial pressure equilibrium constant.

(13)

IONIC EQUILIBRIUM, *pH* AND HYDROLYSIS

Physical Equilibrium

It is the equilibrium between the same chemical species in different phases. e.g.

(*i*) Equilibrium between a liquid and its vapour.

(*ii*) Equilibrium between a vapour and its saturated solution.

Homogeneous Equilibrium

A reversible reaction having all the species in same phase throughout, is called in homogeneous equilibrium.

Here, $\underset{\text{Hydrogen}}{H_2 (g)} + \underset{\text{Iodine}}{I_2 (g)} \rightleftharpoons \underset{\text{Hydrogen iodide}}{2HI (g)}$

Here all reactants and products are gases.

Heterogeneous Equilibrium

A reversible reaction having its species in two or more phases, is called in heterogeneous equilibrium.

Here, $CaCO_3\,(s) \rightleftharpoons CaO\,(s) + CO_2\,(g)$
Calcium carbonate — Calcium oxide — Carbon dioxide

In this reaction $CaCO_3$ and CaO are solids, but CO_2 is a gas.

Ionic Equilibrium

A reversible reaction between species and its ions is called in ionic equilibrium.

e.g. $H_2O\,(l) \rightleftharpoons H^+\,(aq) + OH^-\,(aq)$

Relationship between K_c and K_p

K_c = Equilibrium constant expressed in mol/litre.

K_p = Equilibrium constant expressed in pressures.

$K_p = K_c\,(RT)^{\Delta n}$

where R = 0.08206 litre atm K^{-1} mol^{-1}.

T = absolute temperature.

Δ^n = number of moles of the gaseous products – number of moles of the gaseous reactants in the balanced equation.

Le-Chatelier Principle

It states that if some change is introduced in a system at equilibrium, the system proceeds in such a way that the effect of change is minimised.

Factors influencing equilibrium

(*i*) Concentration of reactant or a product

(*ii*) Reaction volume or applied pressure.

(*iii*) Temperature

Electrolytes and non-electrolytes

Electrolyte: A compound whose aqueous solution or melt conducts electricity, is known as an electrolyte.

Non-electrolyte: A compound whose aqueous solution or melt does not conduct electricity, is known as a non-electrolyte.

Strong electrolyte: A substance which dissociates completely into its ions in an aqueous solution and hence is a very good conductor of electricity, is known as strong electrolyte.

Weak electrolyte: A substance which dissociates to a small extent is an aqueous solution, is known as weak electrolyte.

Degree of dissociation or ionisation (α): Fraction of electrolyte that dissociates into its ions when it is dissolved in water, is known as its degree of dissociation or ionisation, α is 1 for strong electrolytes and less than one for weak electrolytes.

Ionisation Constant of a Weak Electrolyte

According to this law, for a weak electrolyte, the degree of ionisation is inversely proportional to the square root of its molar concentration. It can be proved as follows –

Here,

$$AB + H_2O \rightleftharpoons A^+ (aq) + B^- (aq)$$

$$\Rightarrow \quad AB\ (aq) \rightleftharpoons A^+ (aq) + B^- (aq)$$

Moles before dissociation:	1	0	0
Moles after dissociation:	$(1-\alpha)$	α	α

If C mol/litre is initial concentration of the electrolyte AB.

$$[AB] = C\,(1-\alpha)\text{ mol/litre}$$

$$[A^+] = [B^-] = C\alpha\text{ mol/litre}$$

According to, law of equilibrium,

$$K = \frac{\left[A^+\right]\left[B^-\right]}{[AB]}$$

$$= \frac{C\alpha \times C\alpha}{C(1-\alpha)} = \frac{C\alpha^2}{1-\alpha}$$

where K is ionisation constant for weak electrolytes. For weak electrolytes, $\alpha << 1$, so α can be neglected as compared to 1 *i.e.* $1 - \alpha \approx 1$.

$$\therefore \quad K = C\alpha^2$$

$$\Rightarrow \quad \alpha = \sqrt{\frac{K}{C}}$$

Arrhenius Concept of Acids and Bases

Acid: An acid is a substance which contains hydrogen and which when dissolved into water gives hydrogen ions (H^+). The acid ionizes completely when dissolved in water, is called strong acid. An acid ionizes partially when dissolved in water, is called **weak acid.**

A **weak acid** solution contains unionized molecules in addition to ions. In general,

$$\underset{\text{Acid}}{HA\,(aq)} \rightleftharpoons H^+\,(aq) + A^-\,(aq)$$

Base: A base is a substance which contains hydroxyl group and which when dissolved into water gives hydroxyl ions (OH^-).

A base that ionizes completely into its ions when dissolved in water, is called a **strong base**, and a base ionizes partially when dissolved in water is called a **weak base**. In general,

$$\underset{\text{Base}}{BOH\,(aq)} \rightleftharpoons B^+\,(aq) + OH^-\,(aq)$$

Neutralisation is the process in which hydrogen ions and hydroxyl ions combine to form unionized molecules of water.

$$H^+\,(aq) + OH^-\,(aq) \rightleftharpoons H_2O\,(l)$$

Bronsted-Lowry Concept of Acids and Bases

An **acid** is defined as a substance which has the tendency to give a proton (H^+).

A **base** is defined as a substance which has a tendency to accept a proton (H^+).

Conjugate base: The remainder part of an acid after donating a proton, is called conjugate base.

$$\underset{\text{Acid}}{HCl\,(g)} + H_2O\,(l) \rightarrow H_3O^+\,(aq) + \underset{\text{Conjugate base}}{Cl^-(aq)}$$

Conjugate acid: Base when accepts a proton released by an acid is called as conjugate acid.

$$\underset{\text{Base}}{H_2O\,(l)} + H^+ \text{ (from an acid)} \rightarrow \underset{\text{Conjugate acid}}{H_3O^+\,(aq)}$$

Amphoterism: A particular can behave as an acid by donating a proton in one reaction and as a base in another by accepting a proton. Such a species is called as an amphoteric species. such as water.

$$\underset{\text{Acid}_1}{H_2O} + \underset{\text{Base}_2}{H_2O} \rightleftharpoons \underset{\text{Base}_1}{OH^-} + \underset{\text{Acid}_2}{H_3O^+}$$

Lewis Concept of Acids and Bases

Acid : An acid is a substance or an ion which is capable of accepting a pair of electrons and is called as Lewis acid.

Base : Base is a substance or an ion which is capable of donating an unshared pair of electrons and is called as Lewis base.

Types of Lewis Bases

(*i*) *Neutral molecules* having at least one lone pair of electrons. e.g. NH_3, $R–NH_2$, $R_2–NH$, R–OH, H–OH etc.

(*ii*) All negative ions like F^-, Cl^-, Br^-, OH^-, CN^- etc.

Types of Lewis Bases

(*i*) Electron deficient compounds or molecules having a central atom with incomplete octet : *e.g.* BF_3, $AlCl_3$ etc.

(*ii*) Cations e.g. Ag^+, Cu^{2+}, Fe^{3+}, etc.

(*iii*) Molecules with multiple bonds between two atoms of different electronegativities *e.g.* CO_2.

(*iv*) Molecules whose central atoms has empty d-orbitals, *e.g.* $SnCl_4$, SiF_4, PF_5, PCl_5 etc.

1. $pH = -\log [H^+]$
2. $[H^+] = 10^{-pH}$
3. $pOH = -\log [OH^-]$
4. $pKa = -\log K_a$.
5. $pKb = -\log K_b$.
6. $pKw = -\log K_w$.
7. pH of acidic solution < 7.
8. pH of neutral solution = 7
9. pH of basic solution > 7.
10. $pH + pOH = pKw = 14$
11. K_w is called ionic product of water $= [H^+] [OH^-] = 10^{-14}$ at 25°C. Thus, in pure H_2O; $[H^+] = [OH^-] = 10^{-7}$ molar.
12. **pH of an acidic buffer solution and pH and pOH of an alkaline buffer solution :**

(a) Acidic Buffer : (weak acid and its salt which is a strong electrolyte; e.g. : CH_3 COOH and CH_3COONa);

in general, $H \rightleftharpoons HA^+ + A^-$

$$pH = pKa + \log \frac{[A^-]}{[HA]}$$

(Henderson's equation)

(b) Basic Buffer: (weak base and its salt which is a strong electrolyte; e.g. : NH_4OH and NH_4Cl);

in general, $BOH \rightleftharpoons B^+ + OH^-$

$$pOH = pKb + \log \frac{[B^+]}{[BOH]}$$

13. $K_h = \frac{K_w}{K_a}$, for hydrolysis of anion of weak acid.

$K_h = \frac{K_w}{K_b}$, for hydrolysis of cation of weak base.

$K_h = \frac{K_w}{K_a.K_b}$, for hydrolysis of weak acid-weak base salt.

Where: K_h is hydrolysis constant, K_a is ionisation constant for an acid otherwise called acid dissociation constant and K_b is ionisation constant for a base otherwise called base dissociation constant.

---

(14)

SOLUBILITY AND SOLUBILITY PRODUCT

1. $\text{Solubility } (S) = \dfrac{\text{wt. of solute (in gm)}}{\text{wt. of solvent (in gm)}} \times 100$

$$= \frac{w}{W} \times 100$$

2. For sparingly soluble salt : K_{sp} = Ionic Product.

   Where: K_{sp} is called solubility product.

3. For uni-uni valent or bi-bi valent electrolytes :

   e.g.: AgCl, $BaSO_4$; $K_{sp} = S^2$ *or* $S = \sqrt{K_{sp}}$

4. For uni-bi or bi-uni valent electrolytes:

$$K_{sp} = 4S^3 \text{ or } S = \sqrt[3]{\frac{1}{4} K_{sp}}$$

CHEMO CURIOS

Here are described some important informative clues about the main chemical elements of the Periodic Table and chemistry as a whole. These are regarded as rememberable records of chemistry.

1. Most electropositive element: *Cs* (among stable elements)
2. Most electropositive element which is radioactive in nature: *Fr*
3. Most electronegative element: Fluorine ($En = 4.00$)
4. The second most electronegative element: Oxygen ($En = 3.5$)
5. Most conductive metal : Silver (Ag)
6. Most conductive non-metal : Graphite (element allotrope of carbon)
7. The only liquid metal at room temperature: Mercury (Hg, Z = 80)
8. Chemically most reactive non-metal:

Fluorine

9. The only liquid non-metal : Br
10. Most poisonous element : Plutonium (Pu)
11. Element having lowest I. P. : Cs (among stable elements) I.P. : 3.89 *ev/atom*
12. Element having highest I.P.: He (I.P. = 24.58 *ev/atom*)
13. Element having highest electron affinity : Cl (Ea = 3.61 *ev/atom*)
14. Element having highest electron affinity next to chlorine : Fluorine (Ea = 3.45 *ev/atom*)
15. Least electropositive element: **Fluorine**
16. Platinum (Pt) is called : **White gold**
17. Mercury (Hg) is called : **Quick silver**
18. Petroleum is called : **Liquid gold**
19. 24 carat gold is called : **Pure gold**
20. Graphite is called : **Plumbago or black lead**
21. Graphite is used as **dry lubricant.**
22. Element kept in water : White phosphorus (P_4)
23. Elements kept in kerosene oil : Na, K, Rb, Cs
24. Element sublimes on heating : Iodine
25. Substances sublime on heating (*i*) Nepthalene

(*ii*) Iodine (*iii*) Ammonium chloride (*iv*) Pthalic acid (*v*) Camphor etc.

26. Hydrogen is the only element in the P.T. whose nucleus contains no neutron.
27. The most inflamable gas is hydrogen.
28. Hydrogen is the sole element whose isotopes have separate names and symbols ($_1H^1$: Protium, $_1H^2$: Deuterium, $_1H^3$: Tritium)
29. Approximately 90% of the sun's mass is H_2.
30. Analysis of light emitted by stars indicates that most stars are predominantly hydrogen.
31. In interstitial hydrides hydrogen is present in atomic state. They occupy the vacant spaces of metallic structure.
32. There are only two elements (H and He) in the P.T. that contains zero core electron.
33. Radon (Rn, Z = 86) is the sole inert gas which is radioactive in nature.
34. Non-metals having metallic lusture : Iodine and Graphite.
35. Non-metal which is conductor of electricity : Graphite.
36. Hardest natural occuring substance : **Diamond.**

37. **Trans uranic** or man made elements : After $_{92}U$ i.e. 93 .... onwards.
38. Heaviest natural occuring element: $_{92}U$
39. All metals containing block : *d* and *f*-blocks.
40. Metals, non-metals and metalloids containing block : *p*-block
41. Typical metalloid elements : B, Si, Ge, As and Te
42. Lightest metalloid : **Boron** (3.30 g/cc)
43. Heaviest metalloid : **Tellurium** (6.23 g/cc)
44. Amphoteric metals : Zn, Al, Sn, Pb etc.
45. Elements showing diagonal relationship :

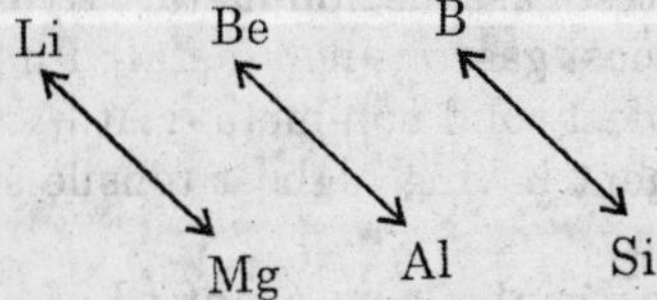

46. **Noble metals :** Au, Pt, Hg, Ag etc.
47. Element having smallest atomic size : Hydrogen
48. Largest atomic size : Cs (among stable elements)
49. Largest cation : Cs^+ (among stable elements)s
50. Largest anion : At^-

51. Smallest anion : F^-
52. A gaseous element having minimum b.p. : Helium
53. Non-metal having highest m.p. and b.p.: Diamond (due to giant covalent structure)
54. Metal having highest m.p. and b.p. : Tungusten (*W*)
55. Carbon has sp^3 hybridisation in diamond
56. Carbon has sp^2 hybridisation in graphite
57. Lightest known element: Hydrogen
58. Lightest solid metal : Li
59. Heaviest solid metal : Os (Osmium)
60. Lightest gaseous non-metal : Hydrogen
61. Heaviest gaseous non-metal : Rn (Radon)
62. Heaviest solid non-metal : At (Astatine)
63. Element having highest tensile strength: Boron
64. Strongest reducing agent : Li (due to its very high +ve oxidation potential)
65. Weakest oxidising agent : I_2 (among stable halogens)
66. Strongest halogen halide reducing agent : HI
67. Most electrovalent compound : CsF
68. Most covalent compound : Diatomic molecules (as H_2, Cl_2 etc.)

69. Most stable carbonate : Cs_2CO_3
70. Strongest base : CsOH
71. Strongest basic oxide : Cs_2O
72. All metaloxides are basic except : ZnO, PbO, Al_2O_3. (amphoteric oxides)
73. All non-metal oxides are acidic except : CO, NO, N_2O (neutral) and H_2O (amphoteric)
74. P_2O_3 and P_2O_5 are solid non-metallic acidic oxides.
75. Natural explosive: NCl_3
76. Artificial explosive : Dynamite
77. Solid CO_2 is called : **Dry Ice**
78. Dry bleacher : Ozone (O_3)
79. Oldest known halogen element : Chlorine
80. Latest known halogen element : Astatine (*At*)
81. Oldest known inert gas : Ar
82. Latest known inert gas : Radon (Rn)
83. *Ortho* and *para* hydrogens are isomers of hydrogen.
84. The most abundant element in the earth's crust : **Oxygen** (49.2% by weight)
85. The second most abundant element in the earth's crust : **Silicon** (25.7% by weight)
86. The third most abundant element in the earth's crust : **Aluminium** (8.1% by weight)

87. The most abundant gas in the atmosphere : **Nitrogen** (78% by volume approx.)
88. Rarest element of the earth's crust : **Astatine** (At)
89. Red variety of HgS is called : **Vermilion**
90. HgS is soluble in aqua-regia.
91. CaF_2 is insoluble in water
92. AgBr is soluble in conc. NH_4OH solution
93. AgI is insoluble in NH_4OH solution
94. $HgCl_2$ (white) is soluble in aqua-regia
95. AgCl (white) is soluble in dilute NH_4OH due to complex formation $[Ag(NH_3)_2]Cl$
96. Hydrolysis by means of an acid is called : **Acidolysis**
97. The process of separation of gases based on the difference in the rate of diffusion is called : **Atmolysis**
98. Thermal decomposition of organic compounds is called : **Pyrolysis**
99. Pyrolysis of alkane is called : **Cracking**
100. Azimuthal quantum number is otherwise called secondary or subsidiary or angular momentum quantum number.
101. Nuclear fission is the basis for the manufacture of **atom bomb**.

102. Nuclear fusion is the basis for the manufacture of **hydrogen bomb**
103. Helium (He) is found in the solar atmosphere
104. C^{14} – isotope is used in **carbon dating process** to determine the age of old wood, rock etc.
105. The man made element made in the first nuclear reactor was : Plutonium
106. Natural radioactivity is always an exothermic process
107. Radioactivity is a first order reaction.
108. The time for complete decay of a given sample of radio-element is practically infinity.
109. All elements after the atomic number 83 are radioactive.
     N.B.: Elements with atomic number 43 and 61 are also radioactive.
110. D_2O (heavy water) is used as coolant in nuclear reactors.
111. Polonium has **27 isotopes**, more than any other element.
112. **Positron** ($_{+1}e^0$) is the **anti particle** of electron ($_{-1}e^0$)
113. Gamma ray has got no charge and no mass.

114. β-particle is equivalent to electron
115. α-particle ($_2He^4$) is equivalent to helium nucleus.
116. Atomic weights of almost all the elements are fractional. (Try to explain)
117. 0.529 Å is called the one atomic unit of length and is equal to **Bohr radius**.
118. Inside an atom, the energy of electron is always negative. (Try to explain)
119. At infinity, the energy of electron is zero.
120. Particle nature of electron is supported by photoelectric effect experiment.
121. Electron has dual (particle as well as wave) nature.
122. **Stern-Gerlach** experiment provides an experimental proof of the fact that angular momentum of electron is quantized.
123. Valency of an element is always +ve and whole number.
124. The **Vander Waal's radius** (non bonded radius) of an element is always greater than the **covalent radius**.
125. Co-ordinate bond is otherwise called **dative bond** or **co-ionic bond** or **semi-polar bond**.
126. Ionic compounds do not exhibit space isomerism.

127. Fe (iron) in solid state has both electrostatic and covalent bonds.
128. Molecule formed by like atoms but polar: O_3 (ozone)
129. Compound containing polar bond but is non-polar: CO_2 (due to its linear structure)
130. It seems that the oxidation number of sulphur in $H_2S_2O_8$ (peroxy di sulphuric acid) is +7, but actually it is +6 (due to presence of two peroxide linkages)
131. Interstitial hydrides are non-stoichiometric, because its composition changes with temperature and pressure
132. The oxidation number of N in N_2 is zero but, its valency is 3. (Try to explain)
133. Valency of C in $C_{12}H_{22}O_{11}$ is +4 but, its oxidation number is zero.
134. **Alchemy:** is chemistry of the middle ages, the chief aim of which was to discover how to change ordinary metal into gold.
135. **Amalgam:** is an alloy with mercury as one of the metals.
136. **Salinometer:** is an instrument for measuring the salinity of a solution.
137. Platinum is called: **Adam's Catalyst**
138. **Albamine** is the old name for astatine.

139. Lead acetate $[Pb(CH_3COO)_2]$ is called : **Sugar of lead** or **INORGANIC SALT**
140. H_2SO_4 is known as **Oil of vitriol** or **Battery acid**
141. An explosive mixture of T.N.T and NH_4NO_3 is called : **AMATOL**
142. An explosive mixture of NH_4NO_3 and Al-metal powder is called : **AMMONAL**
143. **Anthracite** is a variety of coal of high quality.
144. The lowest rank of coal is called : **Lignite**
145. Conc. HNO_3 is also called : **Aqua Fortis**
146. Peroxy disulphuric acid $(H_2S_2O_8)$ is called : **Marshal's acid**
147. Fuming sulphuric acid $(H_2S_2O_7)$ is also called : **Oleum** or **Nordhausen acid**
148. Hydrocyanic acid (HCN) is also called : **Prussic acid**
149. Peroxy mono sulphuric acid (H_2SO_5) is also called : **Caro's acid**
150. K_2CO_3 is called : **Potash** or **PEARL ASH**
151. $CaCO_3$ is called : **Iceland spar**
152. Deposits of impure $CaCO_3$ is called : **Coral**
153. $Ca_3(PO_4)_2$ is called : **Bone ash**
154. Animal charcoal is called : **Bone black**
155. **BATH SALT** : $Na_2CO_3 . NaHCO_3 . 2H_2O$

156. **HAIR SALT** : $Al_2(SO_4)_3.18H_2O$ (alunogenite)
157. **Brunswick green**: $CuCl_2.3Cu(OH)_2$
158. Green vitriol ($FeSO_4.7H_2O$) is also called: **Copperas**
159. Iron pyrites (FeS_2) is called : **Fool's gold** because it has a brassy yellow colour.
160. A black impure variety of diamond is called: **CARBONADO**
161. Mother liquor after crystallisation of NaCl from sea water is called : **Bittern**
162. **Turnbull's blue**: It is Ferrous ferricyanide $Fe_3[Fe(CN)_6]_2$
163. Potassium cyanide (KCN) is extremely poisonous.
164. **NMR** is the abbreviated form of **Nuclear Magnetic Resonance.**
165. **ESR** is the abbreviated form of **Electron Spin Resonance.**
166. **ESR** is also called **Electron Paramagnetic Resonance (EPR)**
167. **LPG** is the abbreviation of **Liquid Petroleum Gas.**
168. **MIC** is the abbreviation of **Methyl isocyanate** : a poisonous gas.
169. Generally organic compounds are covalent.

170. Oldest known organic acid : Acetic acid (CH_3COOH)
171. Element having maximum power of catenation : Carbon
172. The main constituent of **Marsh gas** is : Methane
173. General formula for alkane is : C_nH_{2n+2}
174. General formula for alkene is : C_nH_{2n}
175. General formula for alkyne is : C_nH_{2n-2}
176. General formula for aldehyde is : $C_nH_{2n}O$
177. General formula for organic acid is : $C_nH_{2n}O_2$
178. Alkanes are also called as **Paraffins**
179. Alkenes are also called as **Olefines**
180. Ethylene (ethene) is also called as **Olefiant gas**
181. Ethylene is used to promote the rate of ripening of fruits.
182. **Oxy-acetylene flame** is used for cutting and welding of metals.
183. **Staggered** form of **rotational** or **conformational** isomers is more stable than eclipsed form.
184. Only three organic groups (ether, ketone and amine) can exhibit the phenomenon of **metamerism**.

185. Phenol (C_6H_5OH) is also called **carbolic acid.**
186. Phenol is acidic due to **resonance effect.**
187. **Dutch liquid**: It is ethylene dichloride.
188. **Ethyl fluid**: It is a solution of $Pb(C_2H_5)_4$ and $C_2H_4Br_2$: used as an **antiknock** compound in motor fuel.
189. **Petroleum** is also called **mineral oil** or **rock oil** or **crude oil.**
190. Methyl alcohol (CH_3OH) is also known as **wood alcohol** or **wood naptha** or **wood spirit.**
191. **Ethyl alcohol** is also known as **Grain alcohol.**
192. Nitrobenzene ($C_6H_5NO_2$) is also known as **Oil of mirbane.**
193. **SALOL** : It is phenyl salicylate : used as an internal antiseptic.
194. Methyl salicylate is also known as **OIL OF WINTERGREEN.**
195. 40% aqueous solution of formaldehyde is called as **Formalin** and is used as preservatives.
196. 100% pure ethyl alcohol is known as **absolute alcohol.**
197. **Commercial alcohol (Rectified spirit)** is a mixture of 95.6% ethyl alcohol and 4.4% water.

198. **Wines** contain approx. 12% ethyl alcohol.
199. **Beers** contain approx. 4% ethyl alcohol.
200. **Whiskey and brandy** contain approx. 40-50% ethyl alcohol.
201. **Power alcohol:** It is a mixture of benzenes, petrol and ethyl alcohol.
202. **Methylated Spirit** or **Denatured Alcohol** : Ethyl alcohol containing about 4% methyl alcohol with traces of acetone or pyridine and some colouring matter ($CuSO_4$) is known as methylated spirit or denatured alcohol.
203. **Glacial Acetic Acid:** It is pure anhydrous acetic acid.
204. **Vinegar:** It is 10% acetic acid solution.
205. **Paper:** It is pure cellulose $(C_6H_{10}O_5)_n$.
206. **Freon (CF_2Cl_2)** is used as refrigerant.
207. **Tel** $(C_2H_5)_4Pb$ is an antiknock compound and is used in petrol.
208. **Mendrax** is hypnotic drug
209. **L.S.D.**: It is lysergic acid: used as hypnotic drug.
210. **Tincture Iodine**: It is iodine in alcohol : used as an antiseptic.
211. **D.D.T.** : It is para-dichloro-diphenyl-trichloro ethane : used as insecticide.

212. **B.H.C.** (Gammexine) : It is benzene hexa chloride : used as insecticide.
213. **T.N.B.** (meta-trinitro benzene) is more powerful explosive than **T.N.T.** (ortho-para-trinitro toluene)
214. In benzene, carbon atoms are sp^2 hybridised.
215. Carbon atom has sp^3 hybridisation in methane and ethane molecules.
216. In ethylene molecule, carbon atom has sp^2 hybridisation.
217. In acetylene molecule, carbon atom is in a state of ***sp*** hybridisation.
218. Petroleum is a mixture of solid, liquid, and gaseous hydrocarbons.

DO YOU KNOW?

219. Oxalic acid is obtained from : Cane sugar and Sorrel plant
220. Formic acid is obtained from : Red ants
221. Uric acid is obtained from : Urine
222. Glycerine is obtained from : Olive oil
223. Citric acid is obtained from : Lemon
224. Malic acid is obtained from : Apples
225. Lactic acid is obtained from : Sour milk

16

SOME EMINENT CHEMISTS AND THEIR DISCOVERIES

1. Law of conservation of Mass : **Lavoisier**
2. Law of constant (definite) Proportion : **Proust**
3. Law of Multiple Proportion : **Dalton**
4. Law of Reciprocal Proportion or Law of Equivalent Proportion : **Rickter**
5. Law of Gaseous Volume : **Gay Lussac**
6. Electron : **J.J. Thomson**
7. Proton : **Goldstein**
8. Neutron : **James Chadwick**
9. Positron : **Wilson**
10. Neutrino : **Wilson**
11. Positive Meson : **Carl Anderson**
12. Negative Meson : **Carl Anderson**
13. Meson field theory : **H. Yukawa**

14. Nuclear theory : **Rutherford**
15. Atomic theory : **Dalton**
16. Atomic theory (based on quantum theory) : **Neils Bohr**
17. Quantum theory : **Max Planck**
18. Atomic Number : **Moseley**
19. Quantisation of angular momentum : **Stern-Gerlach** [Experimental proof]
20. Wave nature of electrons first suggested by : **L. de Broglie**
21. Wave nature of electron (experimental proof) : **Davison and Germer**
22. Dual nature of electron : **L. de Broglie**
23. Mass - Energy Relation ($E = mc^2$) : **Albert Einstein**
24. Photoelectric Effect : **Albert Einstein**
25. Theory of Relativity : **Albert Einstein**
26. Mass spectrum : **Aston**
27. Mass spectrograph : **Aston**
28. Hund's Rule of Spin Multiplicity : **Hund**
29. Pauli's Exclusion Principle : **Pauli**
30. Uncertainty Principle : **Heisenberg**
31. Wave Equation for Electrons : **Schrodinger**
32. Molecule : **Avogadro**
33. Avogadro's Hypothesis : **Avogadro**
34. Becquerel rays or (radioactive rays) : **Henry Becquerel**

35. Radioactivity : **Henry Becquerel**
36. Radium : **Marie Curie**
37. Artificial Radioactivity : **Irene Curie and Fedric Joliot**
38. Group displacement law : **Fajans, Russel and Soddy**
39. **Nuclear Fission** : **Otto Hahn** and **Strassmann**
40. Trans uranic Elements : **Seaborg**
41. Law of diffusion of gases : **Graham**
42. Boyle's law : **Robert Boyle**
43. Charles's law : **Charles**
44. Law of Partial pressures : **Dalton**
45. Theory of Electrovalency : **Kossel**
46. Theory of Covalency : **G. N. Lewis**
47. Octet Rule : **G.N. Lewis**
48. Theory of hybridisation : **L. Pauling**
49. Valence bond theory : **First put forward by *Heitler* and *London* and further extension by *Slater* and *Pauling*.**
50. Periodic classification : **D. I. Mendeleef**
51. Atomic Volume Curve : **Lothermeyer**
52. Dobereiner's triads : **Dobereiner**
53. Law of Octaves : **Newland**
54. Modern Periodic Law : **Moseley**
55. Modern concept of acids and bases : **Bronsted and Lowry**

56. *pH* Scale : **S.P. Sorensen**
57. Law of Mass Action : **Guldberg and Wage**
58. Le Chatelier's Principle : **Le Chatelier**
59. Berzelius Hypothesis : **Berzelius**
60. Catalysis : **Berzelius**
61. Laws of Electrolysis : **Faraday**
62. Activation Energy : **Arrhenius**
63. Theory of Ionization (Ionic theory) : **Arrhenius**
64. Measurement of osmotic pressure : **Berkeley**
65. Dilution Law : **Ostwald**
66. Preparation of Colloids by electro-dispersion or Arc Method : **Bredig**
67. Gold Number : **Zsigmondy**
68. Tyndal Effect : **Tyndal**
69. Brownian Movement : **Robert Brown**
70. Hess' Law of constant heat summation : **G.H. Hess**
71. Oxygen gas : **Priestley**
72. Hydrogen gas : **Cavendish**
73. Inert Gas : **Ramsay**
74. Helium : **Frankland and Lockyer**
75. Synthesis of Ammonia : **Haber**
76. Synthesis of HNO_3 from ammonia : **Ostwald**

77. Manufacture of HNO_3 from air : **Birkland**
78. Manufacture of steel : **Bessemer**
79. Sulphur : **Frasch**
80. Heavy Water : **H. Urey**
81. Strain theory : **Baeyer**
82. Synthesis of hydrocarbons : **Kolbe**
83. Synthesis of Urea : **Wohler**
84. Synthesis of higher alkanes : **Wurtz**
85. Optical Isomerism : **Vant Hoff**
86. Gun powder : **Roger Bacon**

IMPORTANT COMPOUNDS AND THEIR FORMULAE

1.	Active nitrogen	Atomic nitrogen
2.	Amatol	80% NH_4NO_3 + 20% T.N.T (explosive)
3.	Alums	$MAl(SO_4)_2.12H_2O$; (M = NH_4^+, Na^+, K^+ etc.)
4.	Arsine	AsH_3
5.	Aqua regia	conc. $1HNO_3$ + conc. 3HCl
6.	Asbestos	$CaMg_3(SiO_3)_4$
7.	Anhydrone	$Mg(ClO_4)_2$
8.	Borane	Hydrides of Boron
9.	Bremstone	S_8
10.	Blue Vitriol	$CuSO_4.5H_2O$
11.	Bleaching powder	Ca (OCl)Cl
12.	Baryta water	$Ba(OH)_2$ solution
13.	Baryta	BaO

14.	Baking powder or soda	$NaHCO_3$
15.	Black jack	Zinc ore
16.	Calgon	$Na_2[Na_4(PO_3)_6]$
17.	Chrome alum	$K_2SO_4.Cr_2(SO_4)_3.24H_2O$
18.	Cerussite	$PbCO_3$
19.	Carborundum	SiC
20.	Cementite	Fe_3C (iron carbide)
21.	Chinese white	ZnO
22.	Caliche	Natural $NaNO_3$ containing $NaIO_3$
23.	Caustic soda	NaOH
24.	Caustic potash	KOH
25.	Corrosive sublimate	$HgCl_2$
26.	Calomel	Hg_2Cl_2
27.	Deuterium	D or ${}_1H^2$ (Isotope of hydrogen)
28.	D.D.T.	*p*-dichloro-diphenyl–trichloro-ethane
29.	Dry ice	Solid CO_2
30.	Flint glass	A natural silicate containing Ca, Si and O_2 as main constituents
31.	Freon	CF_2Cl_2
32.	Ferric alum	$K_2SO_4.Fe_2(SO_4)_3.24H_2O$

33.	Fenton's reagent	H_2O_2 + few drops of $FeCl_3$
34.	Fusion mixture	$Na_2CO_3 + K_2CO_3$
35.	Fehling's solution	A deep blue solution $= CuSO_4.5H_2O + NaOH$ + Na, *K*-tartrate (used for the test of aldehydes)
36.	Fluid magnesia	12% aqueous solution of $Mg(HCO_3)_2$
37.	Feldspar	$KAlSi_3O_8$
38.	Glauber's salt	$Na_2SO_4.10H_2O$
39.	Green Vitriol	$FeSO_4.7H_2O$
40.	Graphite	An allotrope of carbon
41.	Gun powder	75% KNO_3, 12% S, 13% Charcoal
42.	Hydrolith	CaH_2
43.	Heavy hydrogen	D_2
44.	Heavy water	D_2O
45.	Hypo	$Na_2S_2O_3.5H_2O$
46.	Killed spirit	$ZnCl_2 + ZnO$ (Zn-oxy chloride)
47.	Kesserite	$MgSO_4.H_2O$
48.	Leuna saltpetre	Fertilizer $[NH_4NO_3 + (NH_4)_2SO_4]$

49. Lime or Quick lime	CaO
50. Lead of pencil	Graphite (C)
51. Lime water	A clear aqueous solution of $Ca(OH)_2$
52. Laughing gas	N_2O
53. Lurtar caustic	$AgNO_3$
54. Litharge	PbO
55. Lithopone	A white pigment ($ZnS + BaSO_4$)
56. Mortar	A paste of slaked lime and sand (1 : 3) in water
57. Milk of lime	Suspension of $Ca(OH)_2$ in water
58. Minium	Pb_3O_4
59. Massicot	PbO
60. Microcosmic salt	$NaNH_4HPO_4$ (used in the test of silicates)
61. Milk of magnesia	A paste of $Mg(OH)_2$ in water
62. Matte	$Cu_2S + FeS$
63. Mohr's salt	$FeSO_4(NH_4)_2SO_4.6H_2O$
64. Magnesia alba	$2MgCO_3.Mg(OH)_2.3H_2O$
65. Magnesia	MgO
66. Marsh gas	Methane (CH_4)
67. Marble	$CaCO_3$

68.	Muriatic acid	HCl
69.	Nitro chalk	Fertilizer $[NH_4NO_3+(NH_4)_2CO_3]$
70.	Nessler's reagent	Aq. solution of K_2HgI_4 + KOH
71.	Nitrolim	$CaCN_2$
72.	Nascent hydrogen	Atomic hydrogen
73.	Nitrophos	$Ca(H_2PO_4)_2 + 2Ca(NO_3)_2$
74.	Oil of vitriol	Conc. H_2SO_4
75.	Ozone	O_3
76.	Oleum	$H_2S_2O_7$
77.	Phosgene	$COCl_2$
78.	Philosopher's wool	ZnO
79.	Phosphine	PH_3
80.	Pharaoh's serpents	$Hg(CNS)_2$
81.	Pig iron	Impure form of iron
82.	Potas alum	$K_2SO_4.Al_2(SO_4)_3.24H_2O$
83.	Producer gas	A mixture of $(CO + N_2)$
84.	Plaster of Paris	$Ca(SO_4)_2.H_2O$
85.	Quartz	$(SiO_2)_n$
86.	Quick silver	Hg
87.	Quick lime	CaO

88.	Refrigerant	NH_3, CO_2, CF_2Cl_2 etc.
89.	Red lead	Pb_3O_4
90.	Rochelle salt	Sodium potassium tartrate
91.	Rust	$Fe_2O_3 . xH_2O$
92.	Sorel's cement	Mg(OH)Cl
93.	Soda-lime	NaOH + CaO
94.	Soda ash or sal soda	Na_2CO_3
95.	Spathose ore	$FeCO_3$
96.	Salammoniac	NH_4Cl
97.	Slaked lime	$Ca(OH)_2$
98.	Sal volatile (smelling salt)	$(NH_4)_2CO_3$
99.	Spinel	$MgAl_2O_4$
100.	Superphosphate	$Ca(H_2PO_4)_2 + 2CaSO_4$
101.	T. N. T.	Tri-nitro toluene (explosive)
102.	T. N. B.	Tri-nitro benzene (more powerful explosive than T.N.T.)
103.	Tincal	$Na_2B_4O_7 . 10H_2O$
104.	Talc	$3MgO.4SiO_2.H_2O$
105.	Tritium	T or $_1H^3$, an isotope of hydrogen
106.	Vermilion	HgS (red)

107.	Water glass	Sodium metasilicate (Na_2SiO_3)
108.	Water gas	$CO + H_2$
109.	Wrought iron	Pure form of iron
110.	White vitriol	$ZnSO_4.7H_2O$
111.	White lead	$2PbCO_3.Pb(OH)_2$
112.	Zinc white	ZnO

IMPORTANT ORES

	Ore	Formulae	Ore of metal
1.	Alumina	Al_2O_3	Aluminium
2.	Alunite	$K_2SO_4.Al_2(SO_4)_3.4Al(OH)_3$	Aluminium
3.	Azurite	$2CuCO_3.Cu(OH)_2$	Copper
4.	Anhydrite	$CaSO_4$	Calcium
5.	Argentite	Ag_2S	Silver
6.	Brine	NaCl solution	Sodium
7.	Borax	$Na_2B_4O_7.10H_2O$	Boron
8.	Bauxite	$Al_2O_3.2H_2O$	Aluminium
9.	Calaverite	$AuTe_2$	Gold
10.	Chile Saltpeter	$NaNO_3$	Sodium
11.	Cinnabar	HgS	Mercury
12.	Chlorapatite	$Ca_5(PO_4)_3Cl$	Calcium
13.	Calcia	CaO	Calcium
14.	Chalk, Marble, Aragonite, Calcite, Iceland spar, Limestone	$CaCO_3$	Calcium

15.	Carnallite	$KCl.MgCl_2.6H_2O$	Magnesium
16.	Calamine	$ZnCO_3$	Zinc
17.	Cassiterite	SnO_2	Tin
18.	Copper pyrites, Chalcopyrite	$CuFeS_2$	Copper
19.	Copper glance, Chalcocite	Cu_2S	Copper
20.	Cuprite	Cu_2O	Copper
21.	Clay, Kaolin, Chinaclay, Mica, Feldspar	Alumino-silicates	Aluminium
22.	Corundum emery	Al_2O_3	Aluminium
23.	Cryollite	Na_3AlF_6	Aluminium
24.	Diaspore	$Al_2O_3.H_2O$	Aluminium
25.	Dolomite	$MgCO_3.CaCO_3$	Magnesium
26.	Epsom salt	$MgSO_4.7H_2O$	Magnesium
27.	Fluorapatite	$3Ca_3(PO_4)_2.CaF_2$	Calcium
28.	Fluorspar	CaF_2	Calcium
29.	Greenockite	CdS	Cadmium
30.	Gypsum	$CaSO_4.2H_2O$	Calcium
31.	Galena	PbS	Lead
32.	Heavy spar	$BaSO_4$	Barium
33.	Horn silver, Chloragyrite	AgCl	Silver

34.	Haematite (red)	Fe_2O_3	Iron
35.	Nitre	KNO_3	Potassium
36.	Magnesite	$MgCO_3$	Magnesium
37.	Malachite	$CuCO_3.Cu(OH)_2$	Copper
38.	Magnetite	Fe_3O_4	Iron
39.	Pyragyrite	Ag_3SbS_3	Silver
40.	Pyrolusite	MnO_2	Manganese
41.	Rock salt	$NaCl$	Sodium
42.	Schonite	$K_2SO_4.MgSO_4.6H_2O$	Potassium
43.	Sylvanite	$(Ag, Au)Te$	Gold
44.	Sylvine	KCl	Potassium
45.	Trona, Natron	Na_2CO_3	Sodium
46.	Whitherite	$BaCO_3$	Barium
47.	Washing soda	$Na_2CO_3.10H_2O$	Sodium
48.	Zincite	ZnO	Zinc
49.	Zinc blends	ZnS	Zinc

19

SOME IMPORTANT ALLOYS, THEIR COMPOSITIONS AND USES

1. Amalgam	Hg + any other material
2. Alpax	Al + Si
3. Alnico	63% Fe,12% Al, 20% Ni, 5% Co (For making permanent magnets)
4. Bell metal	80% Cu, 20% Sn (Bells, Utencils, Idols, Coins etc.)
5. Bearing metal	82% Sn, 14% Sb, 4% Cu
6. Birmabright	5%Mg, 95% Al
7. Brass	Cu + Zn Household utencils
8. Britannia metal	93% Sn, 5% Sb, 2% Cu

9. Bronze	75% to 90% Cu, 25% to 10% Sn (coins, idols, bells, utencils etc.)
10. Constantan	60% Cu, 40% Ni (electrical apparatus)
11. Common solder	50% Pb, 50% Sn
12. Coinage alloy	75% Cu, 25% Ni (For making coins)
13. Delta metal	Cu + Zn + Fe (ship's propellers)
14. Duralumin	94.4% Al, 4% Cu, Mg, Mn, Si (For making air ships, pressure cookers]
15. Dutch metal	80% Cu, 20% Zn (Golden yellow, Cheap ornaments)
16. Fine solder	67% Sn, 33% Pb
17. German silver	60% Cu, 25% Zn, 15% Ni (utencils)
18. Gun metal	86% Cu, 10% Sn, 4% Zn (for engineering works)
19. Invar	63% Fe, 36% Ni, 1% C (watch pendulum)
20. Manganin	84% Cu,12% Mn, 4% Ni

21.	Mangnelium	85% to 99% Al, 1% to 15% Mg (Aeroplane's frame)
22.	Monel metal	30% Cu, 70% Ni (for making alkali resistant containers)
23.	Munz metal	60% Cu, 40% Zn (coins, tubes, castings)
24.	Newton's metal	Sn + Pb + Bi
25.	Nichrome	Cr + Ni + some Fe (Heater coil)
26.	Pewter	75% Sn, 25% Pb (for metal soldering)
27.	Phosphor bronze	85% Cu, 13% Sn, 2% P
28.	Plumber's solder	70% Pb, 30% Sn
29.	Rolled Gold	90% Cu, 10% Al (cheap ornaments)
30.	Rose's fusible	Bi + Pb + Sn (automatic metal fuses) m.p. = 83°C
31.	Solder	Sn + Pb (For metal soldering)

32. Stainless steel	73% Fe, 1% C, 18 % Cr, 8% Ni (For making automobile parts)
33. Stalloy	Fe + Si
34. Type metal	75% Pb, 20%, Sb, 5% Sn (Compositor's Type)
35. Wood's metal	Bi + Pb + Sn + Cd (For automatic fuses m.p.= 60°C)
36. Y-alloy	Cu + Al

SOME COMMON BOND LENGTHS

1 Å (Angstrom) = 10^{-8} cm

	Bond	Bond length (Å)
1.	C—C (Alkane)	1.54
2.	C═C (Alkene)	1.34
3.	C≡C (Alkyne)	1.20
4.	C—H (Alkane)	1.09
5.	C═C (Benzene)	1.39
6.	O—H (Alcohols)	0.96
7.	C—O (Alcohols)	1.43
8.	C═O (Ketones)	1.21
9.	C—Cl (Chloroalkane)	1.77
10.	N—H (Amines)	1.02
11.	C—N (Amines)	1.47
12.	C═N (Isocyanides)	1.52
13.	C≡N (Cyanides)	1.15
14.	C—Br	1.91
15.	C—I	2.12

16. H—H	0.74
17. N≡N	1.09
18. O═O	1.21
19. F—F	1.42
20. Cl—Cl	1.99
21. Br—Br	2.28
22. I—I	2.67
23. H—F	0.92
24. H—Cl	1.27
25. H—Br	1.41
26. H—I	1.61

MATHS

1

VECTOR

1. A directed line segment is denoted a **vector.**
2. **Vectors** are represented by bold type letters ***a*, *b*, *c*,** ... or $\vec{a}\,\vec{b},\vec{c}$ ...
3. **Modulus** of a vector: If $\overrightarrow{OP} = \vec{a}$, then $|\overrightarrow{OP}| = |\vec{a}| = a > 0$ where a = **magnitude** (a real number and always +*ve*)
4. **Unit vector** in the direction of $\vec{a}$ is $\hat{a}$:

$$\vec{a} = a.\hat{a} \text{ i.e., } \hat{a} = \frac{\vec{a}}{a} = \frac{\vec{a}}{|\vec{a}|}$$

(Thus, a **unit vector** in the direction of a vector is obtained by dividing the vector by its magnitude.)

N.B. (*i*) The unit vector in the direction AB will be denoted by $\overrightarrow{AB}/|\overrightarrow{AB}|$ or $\overrightarrow{AB}/(AB)$.

(*ii*) $\hat{i}$, $\hat{j}$ and $\hat{k}$ are the standard symbols for **unit vectors** along *x*, *y* and *z* axes respectively and $|\hat{i}| = |\hat{j}| = |\hat{k}| = 1$.

5. Position vector of any point P(*x*, *y*) in rectangular co-ordinate system (O-origin),

$\overrightarrow{OP}$ or $P(\vec{r}) = \vec{r} = x\vec{i} + y\vec{j}$,

$|\vec{r}| = r = \sqrt{x^2 + y^2}$ and $\tan\theta = \dfrac{y}{x}$; where

θ = angle between OP and *x*-axis.

(*i*) If position vectors of A and B are

$\vec{r_1} = x_1\hat{i} + y_1\hat{j}$ and $\vec{r_2} = x_2\hat{i} + y_2\hat{j}$

respectively, then $\vec{AB} = \vec{r} = (x_2 - x_1)\vec{i}$

$+(y_2 - y_1)\hat{j}$,

$AB = |\vec{r}| = \sqrt{(x_2 - x_1)^2 + (y_2 - y_1)^2}$ and

$\tan\theta = \dfrac{y_2 - y_1}{x_2 - x_1}$

where θ = angle between AB and *x*-axis.

(ii) If $A(\vec{a})$ and $B(\vec{b})$ are given, then $C(\vec{r})$ which divides AB in $m : n$ (internally and externally respectively)

$$\overrightarrow{OC} = \vec{r} = \frac{n\vec{a} \pm m\vec{b}}{n \pm m}$$ respectively.

(iii) Point $A(\vec{a})$, $B(\vec{b})$ and $C(\vec{c})$ are collinear, If $\vec{r} = x\vec{a} + y\vec{b}$; where x and y are scalars such that $x + y = 1$ or $x\vec{a} + y\vec{b} + z\vec{r} = 0$; where x, y, and z are scalars such that $x + y + z = 0$

(iv) Any vector in three dimension is:

$$\vec{r} = x\hat{i} + y\hat{j} + z\hat{k};$$

$$|\vec{r}| = \sqrt{x^2 + y^2 + z^2}$$ and

$$\hat{r} = \frac{x\hat{i} + y\hat{j} + z\hat{k}}{\sqrt{x^2 + y^2 + z^2}}$$

6. *(i)* If $\vec{a}$, $\vec{b}$ and $\vec{c}$ are three non-coplanar vectors and x, y, z are scalars such that

$x\vec{a} + y\vec{b} + z\vec{c} = 0$, then $x = y = z = 0$

(ii) A vector $\vec{r}$ can be uniquely expressed as a linear combination of non-coplanar vectors $\vec{a}, \vec{b}, \vec{c}$ in the form

$\vec{r} = x\vec{a} + y\vec{b} + z\vec{c}$.

(iii) If $\vec{r} = x_1\vec{a} + y_1\vec{b} + z_1\vec{c} = x_2\vec{a} + y_2\vec{b} + z_2\vec{c}$; then $x_1 = x_2$, $y_1 = y_2$ and $z_1 = z_2$; where $\vec{a}, \vec{b}, \vec{c}$ are non collinear vectors.

(iv) Two vectors $\vec{a}$ and $\vec{b}$ are parallel and collinear when $\vec{a} = x\vec{b}$; where scalar, $x \neq 0$.

(v) Three non-collinear vectors $\vec{a}, \vec{b}, \vec{c}$ will form a triangle when $\vec{a} = \vec{b} + \vec{c}$ or $\vec{b} = \vec{c} + \vec{a}$ or $\vec{c} = \vec{a} + \vec{b}$ or $a+b+c=0$.

7. If $A(x_1, y_1, z_1)$ and $B(x_2, y_2, z_2)$ are given, then

$$|\vec{AB}| = \sqrt{(x_2-x_1)^2+(y_2-y_1)^2+(z_2-z_1)^2}$$
$= d$(say)

Direction cosines of $\vec{AB}$ are $\frac{x_2-x_1}{d}$, $\frac{y_2-y_1}{d}$, $\frac{z_2-z_1}{d}$.

8. Vector equations :

(a) A straight line through $A(\vec{a})$ parallel to $\vec{b}$:

$\vec{r} = \vec{a}+t\vec{b}$; where $P(\vec{r})$ is a point on the straight line.

(b) A straight line through $A(\vec{a})$ and $B(\vec{b})$: $\vec{r} = (1-t)\vec{a} + t\vec{b}$.

(c) Equation of a straight line through $A(\vec{a})$ and || $\vec{b}$: $(\vec{r} - \vec{a}) \times \vec{b} = 0$

(d) A plane through $A(\vec{a})$ || to $\vec{b}$ and $\vec{c}$: $\vec{r} = \vec{a} + s\vec{b} + t\vec{c}$.

(e) Equation of a plane through $A(\vec{a})$ and $\perp^r$ to $\vec{n}$: $(\vec{r} - \vec{a}).\vec{n} = 0$

(f) Work done = $\vec{F}.\vec{AB}$

(g) Area of a triangle = $\frac{1}{2}|\vec{a} \times \vec{b}|$; where $\vec{a}$ and $\vec{b}$ are sides of the triangle.

(h) Area of a parallelogram = $|\vec{a} \times \vec{b}|$, where : $\vec{a}$ and $\vec{b}$ are adjacent sides

(i) Moment of a force = $|\vec{F} \times \vec{r}|$

9. Scalar or dot product :

$\vec{a}.\vec{b} = |\vec{a}|.|\vec{b}| \cos\theta = ab\cos\theta.$

(a) $\vec{a}.\vec{b} = ab$, [when $\vec{a} \parallel \vec{b}$];

$\vec{a}.\vec{b} = 0$, [when $\vec{a} \perp^r \vec{b}$]

(b) when $\vec{a} = \vec{b}$; then $|\vec{a}| = |\vec{b}|$, $\theta = 0°$ and

$\vec{a}.\vec{b} = |\vec{a}|^2 = a^2$

(c) $\vec{i}.\vec{i} = \vec{j}.\vec{j} = \vec{k}.\vec{k} = 1$ and

$\vec{i}.\vec{j} = \vec{j}.\vec{k} = \vec{k}.\vec{i} = 0$

(d) If $\vec{a} = a_1\vec{i} + a_2\vec{j} + a_3\vec{k}$ and $\vec{b} = b_1\vec{i} +$

$+ b_2\vec{j} + b_3\vec{k}$, then $\vec{a}.\vec{b} = a_1b_1 + a_2b_2 +$

a_3b_3 and $\cos\theta = \dfrac{\vec{a}.\vec{b}}{|\vec{a}|.|\vec{b}|}$

$$= \frac{a_1b_1 + a_2b_2 + a_3b_3}{\sqrt{a_1^2 + a_2^2 + a_3^2}\,.\sqrt{b_1^2 + b_2^2 + b_3^2}}$$

10. Vector or cross product :

$\vec{a} \times \vec{b} = |\vec{a}|\,.\,|\vec{b}| \sin\theta.\hat{n}$;

where $\hat{n}$ is a unit vector $\perp^r$ to the plane of $\vec{a}$ and $\vec{b}$.

(a) $\vec{a} \times \vec{b} = 0$ [when $\vec{a} \parallel \vec{b}$];

$\vec{a} \times \vec{b} = |\vec{a}|.|\vec{b}|.\hat{n}$, [when $\vec{a} \perp^r \vec{b}$]

(b) $\vec{b} \times \vec{a} = -(\vec{a} \times \vec{b})$

(c) $\vec{a}.\vec{a} = a^2$ but $\vec{a} \times \vec{a} = 0 \neq \vec{a}$

(d) $\vec{i} \times \vec{i} = \vec{j} \times \vec{j} = \vec{k} \times \vec{k} = 0$;

$\vec{i} \times \vec{j} = \vec{k}$, $\vec{j} \times \vec{k} = \vec{i}$, $\vec{k} \times \vec{i} = \vec{j}$

(e) If $\overrightarrow{OA} = \vec{a} = a_1\vec{i} + a_2\vec{j} + a_3\vec{k}$

$\overrightarrow{OB} = \vec{b} = b_1\vec{i} + b_2\vec{j} + b_3\vec{k}$

and $\angle AOB = \theta$,

then $OA = |\vec{a}| = \sqrt{a_1^2 + a_2^2 + a_3^2}$

$OB = |\vec{b}| = \sqrt{b_1^2 + b_2^2 + b_3^2}$

and $\vec{a} \times \vec{b} = (a_2b_3 - a_3b_2)\vec{i} +$

$(a_3b_1 - a_1b_3)\vec{j} + (a_1b_2 - a_2b_1)\vec{k}$

$$= \begin{vmatrix} \vec{i} & \vec{j} & \vec{k} \\ a_1 & a_2 & a_3 \\ b_1 & b_2 & b_3 \end{vmatrix} \text{ and } \sin\theta = \frac{|\vec{a} \times \vec{b}|}{|\vec{a}||\vec{b}|}$$

11. Scalar triple product :

If $\vec{a} = a_1\vec{i} + a_2\vec{j} + a_3\vec{k}$, $\vec{b} = b_1\vec{i} + b_2\vec{j}$ $+ b_3\vec{k}$ and $\vec{c} = c_1\vec{i} + c_2\vec{j} + c_3\vec{k}$ and $\theta =$ angle between $\vec{b}$ and $\vec{c}$, then

$$\vec{a}.(\vec{b} \times \vec{c}) = \vec{a}.(|\vec{b}||\vec{c}| \sin\theta\, \hat{n})$$

$$= \begin{vmatrix} a_1 & a_2 & a_3 \\ b_1 & b_2 & b_3 \\ c_1 & c_2 & c_3 \end{vmatrix}$$

12. Properties scalar triple product:

(i) A cyclic permutation of $\vec{a}$, $\vec{b}$, $\vec{c}$ does not change the value of the scalar triple product $[\vec{a}\ \vec{b}\ \vec{c}]$ but an anticycle permutation changes its sign only but not its magnitude.

i.e. $[\vec{a}\ \vec{b}\ \vec{c}] = [\vec{b}\ \vec{c}\ \vec{a}] = [\vec{c}\ \vec{a}\ \vec{b}]$

but $[\vec{a}\ \vec{b}\ \vec{c}] = -[\vec{a}\ \vec{c}\ \vec{b}]$ etc.

(ii) The position of dot and cross can be interchanged keeping the same cyclic order of vectors *i.e.*,

$$[\vec{a}\ \vec{b}\ \vec{c}] = \vec{a}.(\vec{b} \times \vec{c}) = (\vec{a} \times \vec{b}).\vec{c}$$

(iii) $[\vec{i}, \vec{j}, \vec{k}] = 1$

(iv) If λ is a scalar, then $[\lambda \vec{a}, \vec{b}, \vec{c}] = \lambda[\vec{a}, \vec{b}, \vec{c}]$

(v) $[\vec{a}+\vec{d}, \vec{b}, \vec{c}] = [\vec{a}, \vec{b}, \vec{c}] + [\vec{d}, \vec{b}, \vec{c}]$

(vi) The value of a scalar triple product is zero, if two of its vectors are parallel

i.e., If $\vec{a} \parallel \vec{b}$ then $[\vec{a}\ \vec{b}\ \vec{c}] = 0$

In particular $[\vec{a}, \vec{a}, \vec{b}] = 0$

13. Vector triple product : If $\vec{a}, \vec{b}, \vec{c}$ are three vectors then $\vec{a} \times (\vec{b} \times \vec{c})$ is a vector quantity and is called the vector triple product of the three vectors, and is denoted by $(\vec{a}\ \vec{b}\ \vec{c})$ or $(\vec{a}, \vec{b}, \vec{c})$.

(i) $\vec{a} \times (\vec{b} \times \vec{c}) = (\vec{a}.\vec{c})\vec{b} - (\vec{a}.\vec{b})\vec{c}$ and

$(\vec{a} \times \vec{b}) \times \vec{c} = (\vec{c}.\vec{a})\vec{b} - (\vec{c}.\vec{b})\vec{a}$

(ii) $\vec{a} \times (\vec{b} \times \vec{c}) \neq (\vec{a} \times \vec{b}) \times \vec{c}$

14. Scalar product of four vectors:

If $\vec{a}, \vec{b}, \vec{c}$ and $\vec{d}$ are four vectors then $(\vec{a} \times \vec{b}).(\vec{c} \times \vec{d})$ is called the scalar product of four vectors.

15. Lagranges Identity:

$$(\vec{a} \times \vec{b}).(\vec{c} \times \vec{d}) = \begin{vmatrix} \vec{a}.\vec{c} & \vec{a}.\vec{d} \\ \vec{b}.\vec{c} & \vec{b}.\vec{d} \end{vmatrix}$$

$$= (\vec{a}.\vec{c})(\vec{b}.\vec{d}) - (\vec{a}.\vec{d})(\vec{b}.\vec{c})$$

16. Vector product of four vectors: If $\vec{a}. \vec{b}, \vec{c}, \vec{d}$ are four vectors, then $(\vec{a} \times \vec{b}) \times (\vec{c} \times \vec{d})$ is called the vector product of four vectors.

$$(\vec{a} \times \vec{b}) \times (\vec{c} \times \vec{d})$$

$$= [\vec{a}\ \vec{b}\ \vec{d}]\vec{c} - [\vec{a}\ \vec{b}\ \vec{c}]\vec{d}$$

$$= [\vec{a}\ \vec{c}\ \vec{d}]\vec{b} - [\vec{b}\ \vec{c}\ \vec{d}]\vec{a}$$

Therefore, any four vectors $\vec{a}, \vec{b}, \vec{c}, \vec{d}$

$$[\vec{b}\ \vec{c}\ \vec{d}]\vec{a} - [\vec{a}\ \vec{c}\ \vec{d}]\vec{b} + [\vec{a}, \vec{b}, \vec{d}]\vec{c} - [\vec{a}\ \vec{b}\ \vec{c}]\vec{d} = 0$$

17. Application of vectors to Geometry

(a) Vector equation of a straight line passing through a point $\vec{a}$ and parallel to $\vec{b}$ is, $\vec{r} = \vec{a} + t\vec{b}$, where t is an arbitrary constant.

(b) Vector equation of a straight line passing through two points $\vec{a}$ and $\vec{b}$ is $\vec{r} = \vec{a} + t(\vec{b} - \vec{a})$, where t is an arbitrary constant.

(c) Vector equation of a plane passing through the point $\vec{a}$ and parallel to two given vectors $\vec{b}$ and $\vec{c}$ is $\vec{r} = \vec{a} + s\vec{b} + t\vec{c}$, where t and s are arbitrary constants.

or $[\vec{r}\ \vec{b}\ \vec{c}] = [\vec{a}\ \vec{b}\ \vec{c}]$

(d) Vector equation of a plane passing through the points $\vec{a}, \vec{b}, \vec{c}$ is

$\vec{r} = (1 - s - t)\vec{a} + s\vec{b} + t\vec{c}$, where s and t are arbitrary constants.

or $\vec{r}.(\vec{b}\times\vec{c} + \vec{c}\times\vec{a} + \vec{a}\times\vec{b}) = [\vec{a}\ \vec{b}\ \vec{c}]$

(e) Vector equation of the plane passing through a point $\vec{a}$ and perpendicular to $\vec{n}$ is $\vec{r}.\vec{n} = \vec{a}.\vec{n}$

N.B. Perpendicular distance of the plane from the origin $= (\vec{a}.\vec{n})|\vec{n}|$.

(f) Perpendicular distance of a point $P(\vec{r})$ from the line passing through $\vec{a}$ and parallel to $\vec{b}$ is given by

$$\text{PM} = \frac{|(\vec{r} - \vec{a}) \times \vec{b}|}{|\vec{b}|} \text{ or,}$$

$$\text{PM} = \left[(\vec{r} - \vec{a})^2 - \left\{ (\vec{r} - \vec{a}) . \vec{b} \, |\vec{b}| \right\}^2 \right]^{1/2}$$

(g) Perpendicular distance of a point $P(\vec{r})$ from a plane passing through the point $\vec{a}$ and parallel to $\vec{b}$ and $\vec{c}$ is given by

$$\text{PM} = \frac{(\vec{r} - \vec{a}).(\vec{b} \times \vec{c})}{|\vec{b} \times \vec{c}|}$$

(h) Perpendicular distance of a point $P(\vec{r})$ from a plane passing through the points $\vec{a}$, $\vec{b}$, and $\vec{c}$ is given by

$$\text{PM} = \frac{(\vec{r} - \vec{a}).(\vec{b} \times \vec{c} + \vec{c} \times \vec{a} + \vec{a} \times \vec{b})}{|\vec{b} \times \vec{c} + \vec{c} \times \vec{a} + \vec{a} \times \vec{b}|}$$

(i) Shortest distance between two non-intersecting lines

$\vec{r} = \vec{a} + t\vec{c}$ is given by

$$PQ = \frac{|\vec{b} - \vec{a}, \vec{c}, \vec{d}|}{|\vec{c} \times \vec{d}|}$$

(*j*) Vector equation of the bisector of the angle between the lines intersecting at the point $\vec{a}$ and parallel to $\vec{b}$ and $\vec{c}$ respectively is

$\vec{r} = \vec{a} + t[\vec{b}/|\vec{b}| + \vec{c}/|\vec{c}|]$,

where t is an arbitrary constant.

N.B : $\hat{a} + \hat{b}$ is a vector along the bisector of the angle between the vectors $\vec{a}$ and $\vec{b}$.

2

PERMUTATIONS AND COMBINATIONS

1. **Fundamental principles**

   (a) If one work can be done in m ways and (after it has been done in any one way) a second work can be done in n ways, then both first and second work can be done in $m \times n$ ways.

   (b) Suppose a work A can occur in m ways and B can occur in n ways and both cannot occur simultaneously.
   Then A or B (at least one of them) can occur in $(m + n)$ ways.

   (c) If a problem deals with only selection, it is a problem of *combination*; and selection with arrangement is a problem of *permutation*.

2. No. of permutation of n different things, taken r at a time :

$$^{n}P_{r} = \frac{\underline{|n}}{\underline{|n-r}} = \frac{n!}{(n-r)!}$$

3. Number of permutation of n things, when p are of one kind, q of another kind and rest all different; taken all at a time

$$= \frac{\underline{|n}}{\underline{|p}\,\underline{|q}} = \frac{n!}{p!q!}$$

4. Number of permutation of n different things, taken r at a time; when things may be repeated once, twice, ... r times $= n^r$.
5. Number of arrangements of n different things in a circle $= \underline{|n-1} = (n-1)!$
6. Number of combination (selection) of n different things, taken r at a time:

$$^{r}C_{r} = \frac{\underline{|n}}{\underline{|r}\,\underline{|n-r}} = \frac{n!}{r!(n-r)!}$$

7. Number of selection of n different things, when one has a choice to select 0, 1, 2, ... n things $= 2^n$
8. Number of selection of n different things, when at least one thing is to be selected $= 2^n - 1$.

9. Number of selection of n similar things, when one has a choice to select 0, 1, 2, 3 .... n things = $(n + 1)$.
10. Number of selection of n similar things, when at least one thing to be selected = $(n + 1) - 1$.
11. Number of combination of n different things taken r at a time when any object may be repeated any number of times.
coeff. of x^r in $(1 + x + x^2 + ... + x^r + ...)^n$
= coeff. of x^r $(1 - x)^{-n}$
$= {}^{n+r-1}C_r$.
12. Number of combination of n different things taken r at a time when p particular things always occur
$= {}^{(n-p)}C_{(r-p)}$.
13. The number of permutations of n different things taken r at a time when p particular things always occur
$= {}^{(n-p)}C_{(r-p)}.r\,!$
14. Number of combination of n different things taken r at a time when p particular things never occur = ${}^{(n-p)}C_r$
15. Number of permutations (arrangements) of n different things taken r at a time when p particular things never occur = ${}^{(n-p)}C_r.r\,!$

16. Number of permutation of n things taken all at a time when p_1 are alike of one kind, p_2 are alike of second kind, ..., p_r of them are alike of the r-th kind $p_1 + p_2 + \dots p_r \leq n$, and remaining things are all different

$$= n!/\{p_1!, p_2! \dots p_r!\}.$$

17. The number of ways in which n distinct objects can be split into three groups containing respectively r, s and t objects, (r, s and t are distinct and $r + s + t = n_1$) is

given by $^{n}C_{r}.^{n-r}C_{s}.^{n-r-s}C_{t} = \dfrac{n!}{r!.s!.t!}$

18. Division into groups :

(a) Number of ways in which $(m + n)$ things can be divided into two groups or packets containing m and n things

$$= \frac{(m+n)!}{m!.n!}$$

(b) If $m = n$, then number of ways of sub-division into groups or packets

$$= \frac{2m!}{m!m!2!}$$

(c) If 2m things are divided equally between two persons, then the number of ways : $\frac{2m!}{m!m!}$

(d) The number of ways in which $m+n+p$ things can be divided into three groups or packets containing m, n and p things

$$= \frac{(m+n+p)!}{m!.n!.p!}$$

(e) If $m = n = p$, then number of sub-division into packets $= \frac{3m!}{m!.m!.m!.3!}$

(f) If 3m things are divided equally between 3 persons, then number of ways $= \frac{3m!}{m!.m!.m!}$

19. Derangements : Any change in the given order of the things is called a derangement.

20. If n things form an arrangement in a row, the number of ways in which they can be deranged so that no one of them occupies its original place is

$$n!\left(1-\frac{1}{1!}+\frac{1}{2!}-\frac{1}{3!}+...+(-1)^n.\frac{1}{n!}\right)$$

21. Greater value of ^nCr : ^nC_r is greatest, when

$$r=\frac{n}{2} \text{ if } n \text{ is even}$$

$$r=\frac{(n-1)}{2} \text{ or } \frac{(n+1)}{2} \text{ if } n \text{ is odd.}$$

22. Some other important relations:

(a) $^nC_r = {}^nC_{n-r}$

(b) $^nC_r + {}^nC_{r-1} = {}^{n+1}C_r$

(c) $^nP_r = {}^nC_r.r!$

(d) $^nC_0 + {}^nC_1 + {}^nC_2 + ... + {}^nC_n = 2^n$

(e) $^nP_0 = 1$

(f) $^nP_n = n!$

(g) $^nC_n = 1$

(h) $^nC_n = 1$

(i) $n! = 1 \times 2 \times 3 \times ... \times n$

(j) $0! = 1$, (by definition)

(k) $n! = n(n-1)!$

(l) If $^nC_n = {}^nC_y \Rightarrow$ Either $x = y$ or $x + y = n$

(*m*) The number of circular permutations of n different things taken all at a time $= (n-1)!$

(*n*) The number of arrangements of n persons on a round table $= (n-1)!$

(*o*) The number of arrangement of n flowers to make a garland $= \frac{1}{2}(n-1)!$

---

(3)

BINOMIAL THEOREM

1. $(a+x)^n = {}^nC_0a^n + {}^nC_1a^{n-1}x + {}^nC_2a^{n-2}x^2 + ... + {}^nC_nx^n$.

   Also $(1+x)^n = {}^nC_0 + {}^nC_1x + {}^nC_2x^2 + ... + {}^nC_rx^r + ... + {}^nC_nx^n$.

   $= {}^nC_0x^n + {}^nC_1x^{n-1} + {}^nC_2x^{n-2} + ... + {}^nC_rx^{n-r} + ... + {}^nC_n$.

   where n is a positive integer.

   Here, ${}^nC_0$, ${}^nC_1$, ${}^nC_2$, ..., ${}^nC_n$ are called Binomial coefficients.

   Some important deductions for $(a+x)^n$:

2. General term is $(r+1)^{th}$ term,

   $t_{r+1} = {}^nC_ra^{n-r}x^r$.

3. Number of terms in the binomial expansion $= n+1$.

4. Middle terms in the expansion of $(a+x)^n$:

   (*a*) When n is even, middle term is

   $$\left(\frac{n}{2}+1\right)^{th} \text{ term}$$

(b) When n is odd, both $\left(\frac{n+1}{2}\right)^{th}$ and $\left(\frac{n+3}{2}\right)^{th}$ terms are middle terms.

(c) In any binomial expansion, the coefficient of middle term has the greatest value.

5. ${}^nC_{n-r} = {}^nC_r$ *i.e.*, co-efficient of equidistant terms are equal.

6. If $(1+x)^n = C_0 + C_1x + C_2x^2 + ... + C_nx^n$, then,

(a) putting $x = 1; C_0 + C_1 + C_2 + C_3 + ... + C_n = 2^n$

(b) putting $x = -1; C_0 - C_1 + C_2 - ... + (-1)^n \times C_n = 0$

(c) $C_0 + C_2 + C_4 + ... = C_1 + C_3 + C_5 + ... = 2^{n-1}$

7. For $[x] < 1$;

$$(1+x)^n = 1 + \frac{n}{1!}x + \frac{n(n-1)}{2!}x^2 + \frac{n(n-1)(n-2)}{3!}x^3 + \frac{n(n-1)(n-2)(n-3)}{4!}x^4 \text{ ... to } \infty$$

where n is any rational number.

(a) For $n = -1$; $(1+x)^{-1} = 1 - x + x^2 - x^3 + \dots$ to ∞

(b) For $n = -1$ and $x = -x$; $(1-x)^{-1} = 1 + x + x^2 + x^3 + \dots$ to ∞

(c) For $n = -2$, $(1+x)^{-2} = 1 - 2x + 3x^2 - \dots$ to ∞

(d) For $n = -2$ and $x = -x$; $(1-x)^{-2} = 1 + 2x + 3x^2 + 4x^3 + \dots$ to ∞

8. Some important points : For the binomial expansion of $(x+y)^n$, where n is a positive integer.

(i) The number of terms in the expansion is $(n+1)$

(ii) In each term of the expansion, the sum of the exponents (power of x and y) is n (*i.e.*, each term is of degree n)

(iii) The binomial coefficients of terms from the beginning and the end are equal since ${}^nC_r = {}^nC_{n-r}$.

9. General term in the expansion of $(x+y)^n$: In the expansion of $(x+y)^n$, $(r+1)^{th}$ term denoted by T_{r+1} is given by $T_{r+1} = {}^nC_r x^{n-r} y^r$.

10. To find the middle terms in the expansion of $(x+y)^n$:

(i) If n is even, then there will be only one middle term in the expansion, which is $(n/2+1)^{th}$ term.

∴ The middle term
$= (n/2 + 1)^{th}$ term
$= {}^{n}C_{n/2} x^{n/2} y^{n/2}$

(ii) If n is odd, then there will be two middle terms in the expansion which are $\frac{1}{2}(n+1)$ and $\frac{1}{2}(n+3)^{th}$ terms
i.e., middle terms are

$$T_{(n+1)/2} = {}^{n}C_{(n-1)/2} \cdot x^{(n+1)/2} \cdot y^{(n-1)/2}$$

and

$$T_{(n+3)/2} = {}^{n}C_{(n+1)/2} \cdot x^{(n-1)/2} \cdot y^{(n+1)/2}$$

11. *To find the $(m+1)^{th}$ term from the end :* In the binomial expansion of $(x + y)^n$, the $(m + 1)^{th}$ term from the end $= (n - m + 1)^{th}$ term from the beginning $= T_{n-m+1}$.

12. Number of terms in the expansion of $(x + y + z)^n$, where n is a positive integer, is $\frac{1}{2}(n+1)(n+2)$

13. Properties of Binomial coefficients :

(i) $C_0 + C_1 + C_2 + ... + C_n = 2^n$

(ii) $C_0 + C_2 + C_4 + ... = C_1 + C_3 + C_5 + ... = 2^{n-1}$

(iii) $C_1 + 2C_2 + 3C_3 + ... + {}^nC_n = n.2^{n-1}$
(iv) $C_1 - 2C_2 + 2C_3 - ... = 0$
(v) $C_0 + 2C_1 + 3C_2 + ... + (n+1)C_n = (n+1)2^{n-1}$
(vi) $C_0C_r + C_1C_{r-1} + ... + C_{n-r}C_n = (2n)!/\{(n-r)!.(n+r)!\}.$
(vii) $C_0{}^2 + C_1{}^2 + C_2{}^2 + ... + C_n{}^2 = (2n)!/(n!)^2.$
(viii) $C_0{}^2 - C_1{}^2 + C_2{}^2 - C_3{}^2 + \dots$

$$= \begin{cases} 0 & \text{if } n \text{ is odd} \\ (-1)^{n/2}\, {}^nC_{n/2} & \text{if } n \text{ is even} \end{cases}$$

14. Exponential Series :

(a) $e = 1 + \frac{1}{1!} + \frac{1}{2!} + \frac{1}{3!} + ...$ to ∞

(b) $e^x = 1 + \frac{x}{1!} + \frac{x^2}{2!} + \frac{x^3}{3!} + ...$ to ∞

(c) $a^x = 1 + x\log_e a + \frac{(x\log_e a)^2}{2!} + ...$ to ∞, $(a > 0)$

(d) $e^{-x} = 1 - \frac{x}{1!} + \frac{x^2}{2!} - \frac{x^3}{3!} + ...$ to ∞

(e) $e^{-1} = 1 - \frac{1}{1!} + \frac{1}{2!} - \frac{1}{3!} + ...$ to ∞

(*f*) $e^x + e^{-x} = 2\left[1 + \frac{x^2}{2!} + \frac{x^4}{4!} + \ldots\right]$

(*g*) $e^x - e^{-x} = 2\left[\frac{x}{1!} + \frac{x^3}{3!} + \frac{x^5}{5!} + \ldots\right]$

(*h*) $e + e^{-1} = 2\left[1 + \frac{1}{2!} + \frac{1}{4!} + \ldots\right]$

(*i*) $e - e^{-1} = 2\left[\frac{1}{1!} + \frac{1}{3!} + \frac{1}{4!} + \ldots\right]$

(*j*) For $a > 0$, $a^x = e^{x \log_e a}$

$$= 1 + \frac{x \log_e a}{1!} + \frac{x^2 (\log_e a)^2}{2!} + \frac{x^3 (\log_e a)^3}{3!} + \ldots$$

(*k*) **The value of *e* :** The value of e lies between 2 and 3 *i.e.*, $2 < e < 3$. The value of e upto ten places of decimals is found as $e = 2.7182818284$.

(*l*) $\lim_{x \to \infty} (1 + 1/x)^x = \lim_{x \to 0} (1 + x)^{1/x} = e$

15. Logarithmic series:

(a) $\log 2 = 1 - \frac{1}{2} + \frac{1}{3} - \frac{1}{4} + \ldots$ to ∞

(b) $\log_e(1 + x) = x - \frac{x^2}{2} + \frac{x^3}{3} - \ldots$ to ∞;

$[-1 < x \leq 1]$

(c) $\log_e(1 - x) = -x - \frac{x^2}{2} - \frac{x^3}{3} - \ldots$ to ∞;

$[-1 \leq x < 1]$

(d) $\log_e n - \log_e(n - 1) = \frac{1}{n} + \frac{1}{2n^2} + \frac{1}{3n^3} + \ldots$

to ∞

(e) $\log_e(n + 1) - \log_e(n - 1) =$

$$2\left(\frac{1}{n} + \frac{1}{3n^3} + \frac{1}{5n^5} + \ldots\right)$$

4

COMPLEX NUMBER

1. General form of a complex number is $x + iy$, where, x is real part and iy is imaginary part and $i^2 = -1$
2. $x_1 + iy_1 = x_2 + iy_2$ if and only if $x_1 = x_2$ and $y_1 = y_2$
3. If $x + iy = 0$, then $x = 0$ and $y = 0$
4. Polar or Trigonometrical form of a complex number $x + iy$ is
   $r\cos\theta + ir\sin\theta = r(\cos\theta + i\sin\theta)$
   where $x = r\cos\theta$, $y = r\sin\theta$, $r^2 = x^2 + y^2$ and

   $$\theta = \tan^{-1}\frac{y}{x}$$

   (i) If $z_1 = r_1(\cos\theta_1 + i\sin\theta_1)$ and
   $z_2 = r_2(\cos\theta_2 + i\sin\theta_2)$, then
   $|z_1| = r_1$; $|z_2| = r_2$; arg; $z_1 = \theta_1$ and $\arg z_2 = \theta_2$
   Now $z_1 z_2 = r_1 r_2 \sin(\theta_1 + \theta_2)\cos(\theta_1 + \theta_2)$
   $\therefore |z_1 z_2| = r_1 r_2$, $\arg(z_1 z_2) = \theta_1 + \theta_2$
   Thus, we have $|z_1 z_2| = |z_1||z_2|$, and
   $\arg(z_1 z_2) = \arg z_1 + \arg z_2$

(ii) $(z_1/z_2) = (r_1/r_2)\,[\cos(\theta_1 - \theta_2) + i \sin(\theta_1 - \theta_2)]$ and

$|z_1/z_2| = (r_1/r_2)$ and $\log(z_1/z_2) = \theta_1 - \theta_2$.

(iii) $|z_1/z_2| = |z_1|/|z_2|$ and $\arg(z_1/z_2) = \arg z_1 - \arg z_2$.

5. The number $r = +\sqrt{x^2 + y^2}$ is called modulus of $x + iy$ and is written as $\text{mod}\,(x + iy)$ or $|x + iy|$.
6. The angle θ is called the amplitude or argument of $x + iy$, and is written as $\text{amp}\,(x + iy)$ or $\arg(x + iy)$
7. Principal value of argument is that value of θ which satisfies the two equations.

$$\cos\theta = \frac{x}{\sqrt{x^2 + y^2}} \text{ and}$$

$$\sin\theta = \frac{y}{\sqrt{x^2 + y^2}}$$

8. If $z = x + iy$, then its conjugate $\bar{z} = x - iy$, and $-\pi < \theta \le \pi$
9. Properties of argument :

(a) $\arg(z_1 \times z_2) = \arg z_1 + \arg z_2 = \theta_1 + \theta_2$

(b) $\arg(z_1/z_2) = \arg z_1 - \arg z_2 = \theta_1 - \theta_2$

10. Properties of conjugate :

(a) $z+\bar{z} = 2x \Rightarrow$ a real number

(b) $z \times \bar{z} = |z|^2 \Rightarrow$ a real number

(c) $z-\bar{z} = 2iy \Rightarrow$ an imaginary number

(d) $|z| = |\bar{z}|$; $\overline{z_1 + z_2} = \bar{z}_1 + \bar{z}_2$

(e) $\overline{z_1 \times z_2} = \bar{z}_1 \times \bar{z}_2$ and $\overline{\left(\dfrac{z_1}{z_2}\right)} = \dfrac{\bar{z}_1}{\bar{z}_2}$; $(z_2 \neq 0)$.

11. Properties of modulus of complex number:

(a) $|z_1 \times z_2| = |z_1| \times |z_2|$

(b) $|z_1 \times z_2 \times \ldots \times z_n| = |z_1| \times |z_2| \times \ldots \times |z_n|$

(c) $|z^n| = |z|^n$

(d) $\left|\dfrac{z_1}{z_2}\right| = \dfrac{|z_1|}{|z_2|}$; $(z_2 \neq 0)$

(e) $|z_1 + z_2| \leq |z_1| + |z_2|$

(f) $|z_1 - z_2| \geq |z_1| - |z_2|$

12. Any root of a complex number is also a complex number

13. Cube roots of unity are 1, ω and ω^2. Where if $\omega = \dfrac{-1+\sqrt{3}i}{2}$, then $\omega^2 = \dfrac{-1-\sqrt{3}i}{2}$ and if

$$\omega = \frac{-1-\sqrt{3}i}{2}, \text{ then } \omega^2 = \frac{-1+\sqrt{3}i}{2}$$

(a) $\omega^3 = 1$

(b) $1 + \omega + \omega^2 = 0$

14. n^{th} roots of unity :

(i) The nth roots of unity are $\propto_r = \cos(2\pi r/n) + i\sin(2\pi r/n) = e^{(2\pi r/n)i}$, where $r = 0, 1, 2, \ldots, (n-1)$.

(ii) If $\propto$ is one of the nth root of unity, then $\propto^n = 1$.

(iii) The sum of all n^{th} roots of unity is zero, *i.e.*, $1 + \alpha_1 + \alpha_2 + \ldots + \alpha_{n-1} = 0$.

(iv) The product of all n^{th} roots of unity is $(-1)^{n-1}$ *i.e.*, $1\alpha, \alpha_2 \ldots \alpha_{n-1} = (-1)^{n-1}$

15. Distance between two points: If z_1, z_2 are two complex numbers then the distance between z_1 and z_2 is $|z_1 - z_2|$

16. Point dividing a line segment in a given ratio :

Let $z_1 = x_1 + iy_1$, $z_2 = x_2 + iy_2$ be the affixes of the points A and B respectively, in the argand plane. If λ be a real number $\neq -1$, then there is a unique point C on AB such that AC : CB = λ : 1.

The point C is given by

$$\left(\frac{x_1+\lambda x_2}{\lambda+1}, \frac{y_1+\lambda y_2}{\lambda+1}\right)$$

The affix of C is therefore, $(z_1 + \lambda z_2)/(1 + \lambda)$.

N.B. : The affix of the mid-point of z_1, z_2 is $(z_1 + z_2)/2$

17. If z_1, z_2, z_3 be the affixes of the vertices of a triangle, the centroid of the triangle has the affix $(z_1 + z_2 + z_3)/3$.

18. Three points z_1, z_2, z_3 are collinear if

$$\begin{vmatrix} z_1 & \bar{z}_1 & 1 \\ z_2 & \bar{z}_2 & 1 \\ z_3 & \bar{z}_3 & 1 \end{vmatrix} = 0$$

5

SEQUENCES AND SERIES

1. A sequence is a function defined on the domain N (the set of natural numbers) with co-domain R or C.
   (*a*) If R is the co-domain, it is called real sequence and if C is the co-domain, it is called complex sequence.
   (*b*) If $f : N \to S$ is a sequence, then it is usually written as $\{f(1), f(2), ...\} \equiv \{f(x)\}$
   (*c*) If $t_n = f(n)$, then sequence is also written as $\{t_1, t_2, t_3 ....\} = \{t_n\}$
2. Series : If $(t_1, t_2, t_3...)$ is a sequence, then $S = t_1 + t_2 + t_3 + ...$ is called the corresponding series.
3. If $a, b, c, ...$ are in A.P. ; then $b - a = c - b = ... = d$(common difference); and $la \pm k, lb \pm k, lc \pm k, ...$ are also in A.P.
4. The arithmetic series is $a, a + d, ... , a + (n - 1)d$.

5. The nth term of an A.P., $t_n = a + (n-1)d$.

6. Sum of the first n terms of an A.P;

$$S_n = \frac{n}{2}\{2a + (n-1)d\} = \frac{n}{2}(a + l)$$

where, n = number of terms,
a = first term and
l = last term

7. Arithmetic mean between a and b :

$$A = \frac{a+b}{2}$$

8. Sum of n arithmetic mean between a and b

$$= \frac{a+b}{2} \times n$$

9. Arithmetic means between two given quantities a and b are

$$a + \frac{(b-a)}{n+1},\ a + \frac{2(b-a)}{n+1}, \ldots, a + \frac{n(b-a)}{n+1}$$

where, n = number of means.

10. In an A.P. series, when sum is given, take two terms as $a - d$, $a + d$; Three terms as $a - d$, a, $a + d$; Four terms as $a - 3d$, $a - d$, $a + d$, $a + 3d$; Five terms as $a - 4d$, $a - 2d$, a, $a + 2d$, $a + 4d$: Six terms as $a - 5d$, $a - 3d$, $a - d$, $a + d$, $a + 3d$, $a + 5d$.

11. If $x_1 + x_2 + x_3 + \ldots$ and $y_1 + y_2 + y_3 + \ldots$ are two A.P., then $x_1 \pm y_1, x_2 \pm y_2, x_3 \pm y_3 \ldots$ are also in A.P.

12. In A.P., $a_n = \frac{1}{2}(a_{n-k} + a_{n+k})$ for $k \leq n$.

13. If a fixed number is added *or* subtracted to each term of a given A.P., then the resulting series is also an A.P. and its common difference remains the same.

14. If each term of an A.P. is multiplied by a fixed constant or divided by a fixed non-zero constant, then the resulting series is also an A.P.

15. Geometric progression : If *a, b, c, d* are in G.P., then $\frac{b}{a} = \frac{c}{b} = \frac{d}{c} = r$ (common ratio)

16. The geometric series is $a, ar, ar^2, ar^3 \ldots$

17. The nth term of a G.P., $t_n = ar^{n-1}$

18. Sum of n terms, $S_n = \frac{a(1-r^n)}{1-r}$ or $\frac{a(r^n-1)}{r-1}$

19. The sum of infinite terms of a G.P.,

$$S_\infty = \frac{a}{1-r}\text{; provide } |r| < 1$$

20. Geometric mean between a and b; $G = \sqrt{ab}$

21. Product of n Geometric means between a and $b = \left(\sqrt{ab}\right)^n$

22. Geometric means between a and b are:

$$a\left(\frac{b}{a}\right)^{\frac{1}{n+1}}, a\left(\frac{b}{a}\right)^{\frac{2}{n+1}}, \ldots, a\left(\frac{b}{a}\right)^{\frac{n}{n+1}}$$

where n = number of means.

23. In a G.P. series when product is given, take two terms as $\frac{a}{r}$, ar; Three terms as $\frac{a}{r}$, a, ar; Four terms as $\frac{a}{r^3}$, $\frac{a}{r}$, ar, ar^3; Five terms as $\frac{a}{r^2}$, $\frac{a}{r}$, a, ar, ar^2; Six terms as $\frac{a}{r^5}$, $\frac{a}{r^3}$, $\frac{a}{r}$, ar, ar^3, ar^5, and so on for more terms.

24. Some important facts about G.P. :

(i) If each term of a G.P. is multiplied or divide by some fixed non-zero number, the resulting sequence is also a G.P.

(ii) If $x_1, x_2, x_3, \ldots$ and $y_1, y_2, y_3, \ldots$ are two G.P. then $x_1y_1, x_2y_2, x_3y_3, \ldots$ and $\frac{x_1}{y_1}, \frac{x_2}{y_2}, \frac{x_3}{y_3}, \ldots$ are also in G.P.

(iii) If $x_1, x_2, x_3 \ldots$ is a G.P. of positive terms, then $\log x_1, \log x_2, \log x_3, \ldots$ is an A.P. and vice versa.

25. Harmonic progression : If a, b, c are in H.P., then the reciprocals $\frac{1}{a}, \frac{1}{b}, \frac{1}{c}$ are in A.P.

Hence, $\frac{1}{b} - \frac{1}{c} = \frac{1}{c} - \frac{1}{b}$.

26. Harmonic mean between a and b :

$$H = \frac{2ab}{a+b}$$

27. Sum of reciprocals of n Harmonic means between a and b = $\frac{\frac{1}{a}+\frac{1}{b}}{2} \times n$

28. Harmonic means between a and b are;

$$\frac{ab(n+1)}{a+nb}, \frac{ab(n+1)}{2a+(n-1)b},$$

$$\frac{ab(n+1)}{3a+(n-2)b}, \ldots, \frac{ab(n+1)}{na+b}$$

where n = number of means.

29. If A, G, H are respectively the A.M, G.M and H.M. of two numbers a and b, then

(i) $AH = G^2$

(ii) $A \geq G \geq H$; where, A, G, H are all positive

30. $t_n = S_n - S_{n-1}$

31. Formula for Σn, Σn^2, Σn^3:

(a) $1 + 2 + 3 + 4 + \ldots n = \sum_{n=1}^{n} n = \frac{n(n+1)}{2}$

(b) $1^2 + 2^2 + 3^2 + \ldots + n^2 =$

$$\sum_{n=1}^{n} n^2 = \frac{n(n+1)(2n+1)}{6}$$

(c) $1^3 + 2^3 + 3^3 + ... + n^3 =$

$$\sum_{n=1}^{n} n^3 = \left\{\frac{n(n+1)}{2}\right\}^2 = \left(\sum_{n=1}^{n} n\right)^2.$$

32. $1.2 + 2.3 + 3.4 + ...$ n terms

$$= \frac{\{n(n+1)(n+2)\}}{2}$$

33. Sum of the first n odd natural numbers $= n^2$

34. Sum of the first n even numbers $= n(n + 1)$.

6

QUADRATIC EQUATION AND EXPRESSION

1. General form of quadratic equation is
$ax^2 + bx + c = 0$;
where a, b, c are constant and $a \neq 0$
2. If α and β be the roots of equation $ax^2 + bx + c = 0$;

then, $\alpha = \dfrac{-b+\sqrt{b^2-4ac}}{2a}$ and

$$\beta = \frac{-b-\sqrt{b^2-4ac}}{2a}$$

For solution:

$$x = \frac{-b \pm \sqrt{b^2-4ac}}{2a}$$

3. A quadratic equation has two and only two roots.

4. $\alpha + \beta = \dfrac{-b}{a}$ and $\alpha \times \beta = \dfrac{c}{a}$

5. If α and β be the roots of equation $ax^2 + bx + c = 0$; then $a\alpha^2 + b\alpha + c = 0$ and $a\beta^2 + b\beta + c = 0$

6. The quadratic equation whose roots are α and β, is given by :
$x^2 - (\alpha + \beta)x + \alpha\beta = 0$

7. If a, b, c are real and one of the roots of $ax^2 + bx + c = 0$ is $\alpha + i\beta$; then the other root is $\alpha - i\beta$;
where $\alpha - i\beta$ is complex conjugate of $\alpha + i\beta$,
$i = \sqrt{(-1)}$.

8. If a, b, c are real and one of the roots of $ax^2 + bx + c = 0$ is $\alpha + \sqrt{\beta}$; then the other root is
$\alpha - \sqrt{\beta}$.
where $\sqrt{\beta}$ is irrational.

9. $b^2 - 4ac$ is called the *discriminant* of the quadratic equation; $ax^2 + bx + c = 0$

10. (*a*). If $b^2 - 4ac < 0$; then roots are imaginary and unequal.
(*b*) If $b^2 - 4ac > 0$, then roots are real and unequal.

(c) If $b^2 - 4ac$ is a perfect square; roots are rational and unequal.

(d) If $b^2 - 4ac$ is not a perfect square; roots are irrational and unequal.

(e) If $b^2 - 4ac = 0$; roots are real and equal.

11. Some important propositions:

(i) If α, β are roots of $f(x) = ax^2 + bx + c = 0$, then $f(x) = a(x - \alpha)(x - \beta)$

(ii) The equation whose roots are α, β is $x^2 - (\alpha + \beta)x + \alpha\beta = 0$

(iii) **One common root** : Two quadratic equations $f(x) = a_1x^2 + b_1x + c_1 = 0$ and $g(x) = a_2x^2 + b_2x + c_2 = 0$ has only *one common root* α if $a_1\alpha^2 + b_1\alpha + c_1 = 0$ and $a_2\alpha^2 + b_2\alpha + c_2 = 0$. So by the method of cross-multiplication, we get

$$\frac{\alpha^2}{b_1c_1 - b_2c_2} = \frac{\alpha}{c_1a_1 - c_2a_2}$$

$$= \frac{1}{a_1b_2 - a_2b_1}, \ (a_1b_2 - a_2b_1 \neq 0)$$

Thus, the required condition for one common root is $(c_1a_2 - c_2a_1)^2 = (b_1c_2 - b_2c_1)(a_1b_2 - a_2b_1)$, and if $c_1, c_2 \neq 0$ (*i.e.*, $\alpha \neq 0$), we have

$$\alpha = \frac{b_1c_2 - b_2c_1}{c_1a_2 - c_2a_1} \text{ or } \frac{c_1a_2 - c_2a_1}{a_1b_2 - a_2b_1}$$

(iv) **Both common roots :** Both roots of the equations $a_1x^2 + b_1x + c_1 = 0$ and $a_2x^2 + b_2x + c_2 = 0$ are common if

$$\frac{a_1}{a_2} = \frac{b_1}{b_2} = \frac{c_1}{c_2}$$

(v) If α is a repeated root of $f(x) = 0$, α is also a root of the equation $f'(x) = 0$

(vi) If α is repeated common root of $f(x) = 0$ and $g(x) = 0$, then α is also a common root of the equations $f'(x) = 0$ and $g'(x) = 0$.

12. Quadratic Expression :

(a) $ax^2 + bx + c$ is the general form of quadratic expression and the corresponding equation is $ax^2 + bx + c = 0$

(b) If the roots of $ax^2 + bx + c = 0$ are α and β; then $x - \alpha$ and $x - \beta$ are factors of $ax^2 + bx + c$

(c) Nature of factor of $ax^2 + bx + c$ depends on the nature of roots of the corresponding equations $ax^2 + bx + c = 0$. In other words the nature of factors depends on $b^2 - 4ac$.

(*d*) If $x - \alpha$ is a factor of $ax^2 + bx + c$, then $a\alpha^2 + b\alpha + c = 0$

(*e*) The general expression of second degree in x and y, $ax^2 + 2hxy + by^2 + 2gx + 2fy + c$ is resolvable into two rational linear factors only when,
$abc + 2fgh - af^2 - bg^2 - ch^2 = 0$

(*f*) Maximum and minimum value of $ax^2 + bx + c$:

(*i*) If $a > 0$, $ax^2 + bx + c$ has a minimum value and there is no limit to its maximum value; *i.e.*, maximum value is $+\infty$.

(*ii*) If $a < 0$, $ax^2 + bx + c$ has a maximum value and there is no limit to its minimum value; *i.e.*, minimum value is $-\infty$.

(*iii*) If $\alpha < \beta$, then $(x - \alpha)(x - \beta)$ is positive when $x < \beta$ or $x < \alpha$, and $(x-\alpha)(x-\beta)$ is negative when $\alpha < x < \beta$.

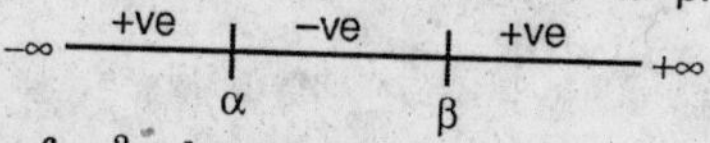

$-\infty$ +ve α −ve β +ve $+\infty$

(*g*) Sign of $ax^2 + bx + c$:

(*i*) When roots of $ax^2 + bx + c = 0$ are imaginary or equal, the sign of $ax^2 + bx + c$ is always according as a.

(ii) When roots of $ax^2 + bx + c = 0$ are real and unequal. (let α and β be the roots). Sign of $ax^2 + bx + c$ is according as a; when x lies outside α and β, and is opposite to that of a; when x lies between α and β.

same as a	opposite of a	same as a

7

TRIGONOMETRY

Some Important Information

1. $\theta = \frac{l}{r}$; where, l = length of arc and r = radius

2. $\pi = \frac{22}{7} = 3.1416$ (approximately)

3. π radian = 180° = 200 grade;
   1 radian = 57° 17' 44.81" (approx)

4. One interior angle of a polygon

   $= \frac{n-2}{n} \times 180°$ where n = number of sides.

5. $\sin\theta = \frac{p}{h}$; $\cos\theta = \frac{b}{h}$; $\tan\theta = \frac{p}{b}$
   where, p = perpendicular, b = base and h = hypotenuse

6. $\sin\theta = \dfrac{1}{\operatorname{cosec}\theta}$; $\cos\theta = \dfrac{1}{\sec\theta}$;

$\tan\theta = \dfrac{\sin\theta}{\cos\theta} = \dfrac{1}{\cot\theta}$

7. $\sin^2\theta + \cos^2\theta = \sec^2\theta - \tan^2\theta = \operatorname{cosec}^2\theta - \cot^2\theta = 1$

8. **Obtuse and Reflex angles :**

(i) $\sin(90° \pm \theta) = \cos\theta$

(ii) $\cos(90° \pm \theta) = \mp \sin\theta$

(iii) $\tan(90° \pm \theta) = \mp \cot\theta$

(iv) $\sin(180° \pm \theta) = \mp \sin\theta$

(v) $\cos(180° \pm \theta) = -\cos\theta$

(vi) $\tan(180° \pm \theta) = \pm \tan\theta$

(vii) $\sin(270° \pm \theta) = -\cos\theta$

(viii) $\cos(270° \pm \theta) = \pm \sin\theta$

(ix) $\tan(270° \pm \theta) = \mp \cot\theta$

(x) $\sin(-\theta) = -\sin\theta$

(xi) $\cos(-\theta) = \cos\theta$

(xii) $\tan(-\theta) = -\tan\theta$

9. **Trigonometrical ratio of compound angles :**

(i) $\sin(A \pm B) = \sin A.\cos B \pm \cos A.\sin B.$

(ii) $\cos(A \pm B) = \cos A.\cos B \mp \sin A.\sin B$

(*iii*) $\tan(A \pm B) = \dfrac{\tan A \pm \tan B}{1 \mp \tan A.\tan B}$

(*iv*) $\cot(A \pm B) = \dfrac{\cot A.\cot B \mp 1}{\cot B \pm \cot A}$

(*v*) $\sin(A + B).\sin(A - B) = \sin^2 A - \sin^2 B = \cos^2 B - \cos^2 A$

(*vi*) $\cos(A + B).\cos(A - B) = \cos^2 A - \sin^2 B = \cos^2 B - \sin^2 A$

(*vii*) $\sin(A + B + C) = \sin A.\cos B.\cos C + \sin B.\cos C.\cos A + \sin C.\cos A.\cos B - \sin A.\sin B.\sin C.$

(*viii*) $\cos(A + B + C) = \cos A.\cos B.\cos C - \sin A.\sin B.\cos C - \sin B.\sin C.\cos A - \sin C.\sin A.\cos B.$

(*ix*) $\tan(A + B + C)$

$$= \frac{\tan A + \tan B + \tan C - \tan A.\tan B.\tan C}{1 - \tan B.\tan C - \tan C.\tan A - \tan A.\tan B}$$

10. Transformation Formulae :

(*i*) $2\sin A.\cos B = \sin(A + B) + \sin(A - B)$

(*ii*) $2\cos A.\sin B = \sin(A + B) - \sin(A - B)$

(*iii*) $2\cos A\cos B = \cos(A + B) + \cos(A - B)$

(*iv*) $2\sin A.\sin B = \cos(A - B) - \cos(A + B)$

(*v*) $\sin C + \sin D = 2\sin\dfrac{C + D}{2}.\cos\dfrac{C - D}{2}$

(vi) $\sin C - \sin D = 2\cos\frac{C+D}{2}.\sin\frac{C-D}{2}$

(vii) $\cos C + \cos D = 2\cos\frac{C+D}{2}.\cos\frac{C-D}{2}$

(viii) $\cos C - \cos D = 2\sin\frac{C+D}{2}.\sin\frac{D-C}{2}$

11. Trigonometrical Ratio :

Angles	*sin*	*cos*	*tan*
0°	0	1	0
15°	$\frac{\sqrt{3}-1}{2\sqrt{2}}$	$\frac{\sqrt{3}+1}{2\sqrt{2}}$	$2-\sqrt{3}$
30°	$\frac{1}{2}$	$\frac{\sqrt{3}}{2}$	$\frac{1}{\sqrt{3}}$
45°	$\frac{1}{\sqrt{2}}$	$\frac{1}{\sqrt{2}}$	1
60°	$\frac{\sqrt{3}}{2}$	$\frac{1}{2}$	$\sqrt{3}$
75°	$\frac{\sqrt{3}+1}{2\sqrt{2}}$	$\frac{\sqrt{3}-1}{2\sqrt{2}}$	$2+\sqrt{3}$

Angles	*sin*	*cos*	*tan*
90°	1	0	∞
120°	$\frac{\sqrt{3}}{2}$	$-\frac{1}{2}$	$-\sqrt{3}$
135°	$\frac{1}{\sqrt{2}}$	$-\frac{1}{\sqrt{2}}$	–1
150°	$\frac{1}{2}$	$\frac{-\sqrt{3}}{2}$	$-\frac{1}{\sqrt{3}}$
180°	0	–1	0
270°	–1	0	∞
360°	0	1	0

$$\sin 18^\circ = \frac{\sqrt{5}-1}{4}$$

$$\cos 18^\circ = \frac{\sqrt{10+2\sqrt{5}}}{4}$$

$$\sin 36^\circ = \frac{\sqrt{10-2\sqrt{5}}}{4}$$

$$\cos 36° = \frac{\sqrt{5}+1}{4}$$

$$\sin 22\frac{1}{2}^{\circ} = \frac{\sqrt{2-\sqrt{2}}}{2}$$

$$\cos 22\frac{1}{2}^{\circ} = \frac{\sqrt{2+\sqrt{2}}}{2}$$

12. General values for Trigonometrical equations :

(i) If $\sin\theta = 0$ or $\tan\theta = 0$, ... then $\theta = n\pi$

(ii) If $\cos\theta = 0$ or $\cot\theta = 0$, then

$$\theta = (2n+1)\times\frac{\pi}{2}$$

(iii) If $\sin\theta = \pm 1$, ... then $\theta = (4n \pm 1)\times\frac{\pi}{2}$

(iv) If $\cos\theta = 1$, ... then $\theta = 2n\pi$.

(v) If $\cos\theta = -1$, ... then $\theta = (2n+1)\pi$.

(vi) If $\sin\theta = \sin\alpha$, ... then $\theta = n\pi + (-1)^n\alpha$

(vii) If $\cos\theta = \cos\alpha$, ... then $\theta = 2n\pi \pm \alpha$

(viii) If $\tan\theta = \tan\alpha$, ... then $\theta = n\pi + \alpha$
where $n = 0, \pm 1, \pm 2, \pm 3, \ldots$

13. Inverse Circular Functions :

(i) $\sin(\sin^{-1}x) = x$

(ii) $\sin^{-1}(\sin x) = x$

(iii) $\sin^{-1}x = \operatorname{cosec}^{-1}\frac{1}{x}$

(iv) $\cos^{-1}x = \sec^{-1}\frac{1}{x}$

(v) $\tan^{-1}x = \cot^{-1}\frac{1}{x}$

(vi) $\sin^{-1}x + \cos^{-1}x = \tan^{-1}x + \cot^{-1}x$

$$= \sec^{-1}x + \operatorname{cosec}^{-1}x = \frac{\pi}{2}$$

(vii) $\sin^{-1}x \pm \sin^{-1}y =$

$$\sin^{-1}\left(x\sqrt{1-y^2} \pm y\sqrt{1-x^2}\right)$$

(viii) $\cos^{-1}x \pm \cos^{-1}y =$

$$\cos^{-1}\left(xy \mp \sqrt{(1-x^2)(1-y^2)}\right)$$

(ix) $\tan^{-1}x \pm \tan^{-1}y = \tan^{-1}\frac{x \pm y}{1 \mp xy}$

(x) $\cot^{-1}x \pm \cot^{-1}y = \cot^{-1}\frac{xy \mp 1}{y \pm x}$

(xi) $\tan^{-1}x + \tan^{-1}y + \tan^{-1}z = \tan^{-1}\dfrac{x+y+z-xyz}{1-yz-zx-xy}$

(xii) $2\tan^{-1}x = \tan^{-1}\dfrac{2x}{1-x^2} = \sin^{-1}\dfrac{2x}{1+x^2} = \cos^{-1}\dfrac{1-x^2}{1+x^2}$.

14. Logarithm:

(i) $\log_a a = 1$

(ii) $\log 1 = 0$

(iii) $\log 10 = 1$

(iv) $\log_a mn = \log_a m + \log_a n$

(v) $\log_a \dfrac{m}{n} = \log_a m - \log_a n$

(vi) $\log_a m^n = n\log_a m$

(vii) $\log_a m = \log_b m \times \log_a b$

(viii) $\log_a b = \dfrac{1}{\log_b a}$

(ix) $Lf(x) = 10 + \log f(x)$ {where, $f(x) = \sin x$, $\cos x$, $\tan x$, $\cot x$, $\sec x$, $\operatorname{cosec} x$}

15. Properties of Triangles:

(i) $a = c\cos B + b\cos C$

(ii) $b = a\cos C + c\cos A$

(iii) $c = b \cos A + a \cos B$

(iv) $$\frac{a}{\sin A} = \frac{b}{\sin B} = \frac{C}{\sin C} = 2R = \frac{abc}{2\Delta}$$

(v) $$\cos A = \frac{b^2 + c^2 - a^2}{2bc}$$

(vi) $$\cos B = \frac{a^2 + c^2 - b^2}{2ac}$$

(vii) $$\cos C = \frac{a^2 + b^2 - c^2}{2ab}$$

(viii) $$\sin\frac{A}{2} = \sqrt{\frac{(s-b)(s-c)}{bc}}$$

(ix) $$\cos\frac{A}{2} = \sqrt{\frac{s(s-a)}{bc}}$$

(x) $$\tan\frac{A}{2} = \sqrt{\frac{(s-b)(s-c)}{s(s-a)}} = \frac{\Delta}{s(s-a)}$$

$$= \frac{(s-b)(s-c)}{\Delta}$$

where $s = \dfrac{a+b+c}{2}$ and

$$\Delta = \frac{bc\sin A}{2} = \frac{ac\sin B}{2} = \frac{ab\sin c}{2}$$

$$\Delta = \frac{abc}{4R} = \frac{1}{2}r(a+b+c)$$

$$= \sqrt{s(s-a)(s-b)(s-c)}$$

(xi) $(\cos\theta \pm i\sin\theta)^n = \cos n\theta \pm i\sin n\theta$

(xii) If in Δ ABC; b, c and $\angle$ B are given, then for ambiguous case : $c > b > c\sin B$.

16. Trigonometrical Expansions :

(i) $\sin\theta = \theta - \dfrac{\theta^3}{\lfloor 3} + \dfrac{\theta^5}{\lfloor 5} - \dfrac{\theta^7}{\lfloor 7} + \ldots$

(ii) $\cos\theta = 1 - \dfrac{\theta^2}{\lfloor 2} + \dfrac{\theta^4}{\lfloor 4} - \dfrac{\theta^6}{\lfloor 6} + \ldots$

8

CO-ORDINATE GEOMETRY

1. Points and Co-Ordinates :

(i) Distance between two points $P(x_1, y_1)$ and $Q(x_2, y_2)$

$$PQ = \sqrt{(x_1 - x_2)^2 + (y_1 - y_2)^2}$$

(ii) Distance between two points $P(r_1, \theta_1)$ and $Q(r_2, \theta_2)$

$$PQ = \sqrt{r_1^2 + r_2^2 - 2r_1r_2 \cos(\theta_1 - \theta_2)}$$

(iii) Co-ordinates of the point which divides (internally) the line joining the points $P(x_1, y_1)$ and $Q(x_2, y_2)$ in the ratio $m : n$, are given by :

$$\frac{mx_2 + nx_1}{m+n}, \frac{my_2 + ny_1}{m+n}$$

(iv) In the case of external division the co-ordinates are

$$\frac{mx_2 - nx_1}{m-n}, \frac{my_2 - ny_1}{m-n}$$

(v) The co-ordinates of the middle point of PQ are :

$$\frac{x_1 + x_2}{2}, \frac{y_1 + y_2}{2}$$

(vi) In a triangle ABC with the co-ordinates $A(x_1, y_1)$, $B(x_2, y_2)$ and $C(x_3, y_3)$, the *centroid* is given by :

$$\frac{x_1 + x_2 + x_3}{3}, \frac{y_1 + y_2 + y_3}{3}$$ and the

incentre is given $\frac{ax_1 + bx_2 + cx_3}{a+b+c}$,

$$\frac{ay_1 + by_2 + cy_3}{a+b+c}$$

where, a, b, c are the sides of the triangle.

(vii) Area of the triangle

$$ABC = \frac{1}{2}\begin{vmatrix} x_1 & y_1 & 1 \\ x_2 & y_2 & 1 \\ x_3 & y_3 & 1 \end{vmatrix}$$

$$= \frac{1}{2}\left[x_1(y_2 - y_3) + x_2(y_3 - y_1) + x_3(y_1 - y_2)\right]$$

The three points : A, B, C will be collinear only when area of the Δ ABC = 0

(viii) The slope (m) of the line joining the points (x_1, y_1) & (x_2, y_2)

$$m = \frac{y_1 - y_2}{x_1 - x_2}$$

2. Equations of straight line :

(i) The standard form

(a) $y = mx + c$

(b) $\frac{x}{a} + \frac{y}{b} = 1$, intercept form

(c) $x \cos \alpha + y \sin \alpha = p$, normal form

(ii) The equation of a straight line which passes through (x_1, y_1) and whose slope is m, is given by :

$(y - y_1) = m(x - x_1)$

(iii) The equation of a straight line passing through two given points (x_1, y_1) and (x_2, y_2) is given by :

$$y - y_1 = \frac{y_1 - y_2}{x_1 - x_2}(x - x_1)$$

(iv) Every first degree equation namely $ax + by + c = 0$, represents a straight line.

(v) The angle θ between the lines, $y_1 = m_1 x + c_1$ and $y_2 = m_2 x + c_2$, is given by :

$$\tan\theta = \frac{m_1 - m_2}{1 + m_1 m_2}$$

(vi) The lines are parallel if $m_1 = m_2$ and they are perpendicular to each other if $m_1 . m_2 = -1$.

(vii) The angle θ between the lines, $a_1 x + b_1 y + c_1 = 0$ and $a_2 x + b_2 y + c_2 = 0$, is given by :

$$\tan\theta = \frac{a_1 b_2 - a_2 b_1}{a_1 a_2 + b_1 b_2}$$

The lines are parallel if

$\frac{a_1}{a_2} = \frac{b_1}{b_2}$ and they are perpendicular to each other if $a_1 a_2 + b_1 b_2 = 0$.

(viii) The equation of the straight line passing through the point of intersection of the lines, $ax + by + c = 0$ and $a_1x + b_1y + c_1 = 0$ is given by $ax + by + c + \lambda(a_1x + b_1y + c_1) = 0$; where : λ is a constant.

(ix) The lines $L_1 = a_1x + b_1y + c_1 = 0$; $L_2 = a_2x + b_2y + c_2 = 0$ and $L_3 = a_3x + b_3y + c_3 = 0$ are concurrent

$$\text{if } \begin{vmatrix} a_1 & b_1 & c_1 \\ a_2 & b_2 & c_2 \\ a_3 & b_3 & c_3 \end{vmatrix} = 0$$

(x) Length of the perpendicular from the point (x_1, y_1) upon the straight line $ax+by+c=0$, is given by: $\dfrac{ax_1 + by_1 + c}{\sqrt{a^2 + b^2}}$.

(xi) The equation of the bisectors of the angle included between the straight lines, $a_1x + b_1y + c_1 = 0$ and $a_2x + b_2y + c_2 = 0$ is given by

$$\frac{a_1x + b_1y + c_1}{\sqrt{a_1{}^2 + b_1{}^2}} = \frac{\pm a_2x + b_2y + c_2}{\sqrt{a_2^2 + b_2^2}}$$

3. Pair of Straight line :

(i) Every second degree homogeneous equation, namely $ax^2 + 2hxy + by^2 = 0$, represents a pair of straight line passing through the origin.

(ii) The angle (θ) included between the lines, $ax^2 + 2hxy + by^2 = 0$, is given by

$$: \tan\theta = \frac{2\sqrt{h^2 - ab}}{a+b}.$$

The lines are perpendicular to each other if $a + b = 0$ *i.e.*, the co-efficient of x^2 + the co-efficient of $y^2 = 0$

(iii) Bisectors of the angles between the lines,
$ax^2 + 2hxy + by^2 = 0$, are given by:

$$\frac{x^2 - y^2}{a - b} = \frac{xy}{h}$$

(iv) The general equation of second degree, $ax^2 + 2hxy + by^2 + 2gx + 2fy + c = 0$ represents two straight lines if, $abc + 2fgh - af^2 - bg^2 - ch^2 = 0$.

(v) The equation of a straight line, joining the origin and the point of intersection

of a straight line and a given curve of second degree is obtained by making the equation of the curve homogeneous with the help of the straight line.

4. Equation of circle :

(i) The equation of the circle whose centre is (0, 0) and radius is a : is given by $x^2 + y^2 = a^2$.

(ii) The equation of the circle whose centre is (α, β) and radius is a : is given by : $(x - \alpha)^2 + (y - \beta)^2 = a^2$

(iii) The equation $x^2 + y^2 + 2gx + 2fy + c = 0$, represents a circle whose centre is $(-g, -f)$ and radius is $\sqrt{g^2 + f^2 - c}$.

(iv) The equation of the circle described on the line joining (x_1, y_1) and (x_2, y_2) as diameter; is given by $(x - x_1)(x - x_2) + (y - y_1)(y - y_2) = 0$

(v) The equation of the tangent at the point (α, β) of the circle $x^2 + y^2 = a^2$; is given by: $x\alpha + y\beta = a^2$

(vi) The straight line $y = mx + a\sqrt{1+m^2}$ or $x \cos\theta + y \sin\theta = a$, is always a tangent to the circle, $x^2 + y^2 = a^2$.

(vii) If a straight line is tangent to the circle, then the length of perpendicular from the centre upon the line is equal to the radius of the circle.

(viii) The equation of the chord of contact of the tangents drawn from (x_1, y_1) to the circle $x^2 + y^2 = a^2$; is given by $xx_1 + yy_1 = a^2$

(ix) The equation of a pair of tangents drawn from the point (α, β) to the circle $x^2 + y^2 = a^2$: is given by $ss_1 = T^2$; where : $s = x^2 + y^2 - a^2$, $s_1 = \alpha^2 + \beta^2 - a^2$ and $T = x\alpha + y\beta - a^2$

(x) The equation of the chord of the circle $x^2 + y^2 = a^2$, whose middle point is (α, β); is given by: $s_1 = T$

(xi) The equation of the polar of the point (α, β) with respect to the circle $x^2 + y^2 = a^2$; is given by $x\alpha + y\beta = a^2$.

9

DIFFERENTIAL CALCULUS

1. Properties of limits :

(*i*) The limit of a constant quantity is the quantity itself

(*ii*) Lt $(u + v)$ = Lt u + Lt v; if Lt u and Lt v exist.

(*iii*) Lt $(u \times v)$ = Lt $u \times$ Lt v; if Lt u and Lt v exist.

(*iv*) $\text{Lt}\,\frac{u}{v} = \frac{\text{Lt}\,u}{\text{Lt}\,v}$; if Lt u and Lt v exist and Lt $v \neq 0$.

(*v*) Limit exists when Left hand limit = Right hand limit; *i.e.*,

$$\underset{x \to a^-}{\text{Lt}}\, f(x) = \underset{x \to a^+}{\text{Lt}}\, f(x)$$

2. $\underset{x \to 0}{\text{Lt}}\, \frac{x^n - a^n}{x - a} = na^{n-1}$; where: n is a rational number

3. $\underset{\theta \to 0}{\text{Lt}} \dfrac{\sin\theta}{\theta} = 1$

4. $\underset{\theta \to 0}{\text{Lt}} \cos\theta = 1$

5. $\underset{\theta \to 0}{\text{Lt}} \dfrac{\tan\theta}{\theta} = 1$

6. $\underset{x \to 0}{\text{Lt}} (1+x)^{\frac{1}{x}} = \underset{x \to \infty}{\text{Lt}} \left(1+\dfrac{1}{x}\right)^{x} = e$

7. $\underset{x \to 0}{\text{Lt}} \dfrac{1}{x} \log(1+x) = 1$

8. $\underset{x \to 0}{\text{Lt}} \dfrac{(1+x)^{n} - 1}{x} = n$

9. $\underset{x \to 0}{\text{Lt}} \dfrac{a^{x} - 1}{x} = \log_e a$

10. $\underset{x \to 0}{\text{Lt}} \dfrac{e^{x} - 1}{x} = 1$

11. $\underset{n \to \infty}{\text{Lt}} \dfrac{x^{n}}{n} = 0 \; [-1 < x < 1]$

12. $\underset{n \to \infty}{\text{Lt}} x^n = 0 \; [-1 < x < 1]$

13. **Indeterminate forms are : 0/0, ∞/∞, 0 × ∞, ∞ – ∞, 0^0, ∞^0 (The forms 0 × ∞, ∞ – ∞, 0^0, 1^∞, ∞^∞ can be reduced to the form 0/0 and ∞/∞)**

14. **L. Hospital's rule for indeterminate forms :**

$$\underset{x \to a}{\text{Lt}} \frac{f(x)}{g(x)} = \underset{x \to a}{\text{Lt}} \frac{f'(x)}{g'(x)} = \underset{x \to a}{\text{Lt}} \frac{f''(x)}{g''(x)}$$

We continue this process till it attains the form [0/0] or [∞/∞] provided the latter limit exists as x approaches a.

15. **Standard derivatives of differentiation:**

(i) $\frac{d(c)}{dx} = 0$

(ii) $\frac{d(x^n)}{dx} = n\, x^{n-1}$

(iii) $\frac{d(x)}{dx} = 1$

(iv) $\frac{d(\sqrt{x})}{dx} = \frac{1}{2\sqrt{x}}$

(v) $$\frac{d(\sin x)}{dx} = \cos x$$

(vi) $$\frac{d(\cos x)}{dx} = -\sin x$$

(vii) $$\frac{d(\tan x)}{dx} = \sec^2 x$$

(viii) $$\frac{d(\cot x)}{dx} = -\operatorname{cosec}^2 x$$

(ix) $$\frac{d(\sec x)}{dx} = \sec x.\tan x$$

(x) $$\frac{d(\operatorname{cosec} x)}{dx} = -\operatorname{cosec} x.\cot x$$

(xi) $$\frac{d\left(e^{mx}\right)}{dx} = me^{mx}$$

(xii) $$\frac{d\left(e^{x}\right)}{dx} = e^{x}$$

(xiii) $$\frac{d\left(a^{x}\right)}{dx} = a^{x}\log_e a$$

(xiv) $$\frac{d(\log x)}{dx} = \frac{1}{x}$$

(xv) $$\frac{d(\log_a x)}{dx} = \frac{1}{x}\log_a e$$

(xvi) $$\frac{d\left(\sin^{-1} x\right)}{dx} = \frac{1}{\sqrt{1-x^2}}$$

(xvii) $$\frac{d\left(\cos^{-1} x\right)}{dx} = -\frac{1}{\sqrt{1-x^2}}$$

(xviii) $$\frac{d\left(\tan^{-1} x\right)}{dx} = \frac{1}{1+x^2}$$

(xix) $$\frac{d\left(\cot^{-1} x\right)}{dx} = -\frac{1}{1+x^2}$$

(xx) $$\frac{d(\sec^{-1} x)}{dx} = \frac{1}{x\sqrt{x^2-1}}$$

(xxi) $$\frac{d\left(\operatorname{cosec}^{-1} x\right)}{dx} = -\frac{1}{x\sqrt{x^2-1}}$$

16. Fundamental theorems on differentiation:

(i) $$\frac{d\{cf(x)\}}{dx} = c\frac{d\{f(x)\}}{dx};$$

where : c = constant

(ii) $$\frac{d\{f(x) \pm g(x) \pm h(x) \pm ...\}}{dx} = \frac{d\{f(x)\}}{dx} \pm \frac{d\{g(x)\}}{dx} \pm \frac{d\{h(x)\}}{dx} \pm ..$$

(iii) $$\frac{d(uv)}{dx} = u\frac{dv}{dx} + v\frac{du}{dx}$$

(iv) $$\frac{d(uvw)}{dx} = uv\frac{dw}{dx} + vw\frac{du}{dx} + uw\frac{dv}{dx}$$

(v) $$\frac{d}{dx}\left(\frac{u}{v}\right) = \frac{v\frac{du}{dx} - u\frac{dv}{dx}}{v^2}$$

(vi) If $y = f(u)$ and $u = g(x)$, then

$$\frac{dy}{dx} = \frac{dy}{du} \times \frac{du}{dx}$$

(vii) Differentiate all the terms of an implicit function with respect to x, and then collect co-efficients of $\frac{dy}{dx}$.

(viii) Whenever the power is variable, take log, and then differentiate, *i.e.*, $y = x^y$.

$\therefore \log y = y \log x$

(ix) $\dfrac{dy}{dx} = \dfrac{\frac{dy}{dt}}{\frac{dx}{dt}}$ [Parametric equation];

Provided $\dfrac{dx}{dt} \neq 0$

(x) $\dfrac{dy}{dz} = \dfrac{\frac{dy}{dx}}{\frac{dz}{dx}}$ $\left[\text{where } \dfrac{dz}{dx} \neq 0\right]$

(xi) $\dfrac{d^2y}{dx^2} = \dfrac{d}{dx}\left(\dfrac{dy}{dx}\right)$

17. More about Tangents and Normals :

(i) Equation of tangent at (x, y) on curve $y = f(x)$:

$$\mathrm{Y} - y = \left(\frac{dy}{dx}\right)(\mathrm{X} - x);$$

where : $\frac{dy}{dx} = m =$ slope of tangent at the point (x, y)
$= \tan \theta$. [θ is the angle which the tangent makes with X-axis], (X, Y) is a new point on the tangent.

(ii) When $m = 0$; Tangent is parallel to X-axis.

(iii) When $m = \infty$; Tangent is perpendicular.

(iv) Equation of normal at (x, y):

$$Y - y = -\frac{1}{m}(X - x)$$

(v) Angle of intersection: For two curves and for two tangents of a curve,

$$\tan \theta = \left|\frac{m_1 - m_2}{1 + m_1 m_2}\right|.$$

18. $\frac{dy}{dx}$ = rate of change of y with respect to x.

19. Some useful formulae of Mensuration :

(i) Volume of sphere $= \frac{4}{3}\pi r^3$;

Surface area $= 4\pi r^2$

(ii) Volume of cylinder $= \pi r^2 h$;
Curved surface area $= 2\pi rh$

(iii) Volume of cone $= \frac{1}{3}\pi r^2 h$;

Curved surface area $= \pi rl$;

Semivertical angle $= \tan^{-1}\frac{r}{h}$;

where : l = slant height $= \sqrt{r^2 + h^2}$

(iv) Area of Parallelogram $= b \times h$;
[b = base, h = height]

(v) Area of Rhombus $= \frac{d_1 \times d_2}{2}$;
[d_1 & d_2 are diagonals]

(vi) Area of Trapezium $= \frac{a+b}{2} \times h$;

where: a and b are parallel sides and h = height.

20. Maxima and Minima

(i) If $f'(c) = 0$ and $f''(c)$ is negative, then $f(x)$ is maximum for $x = c$.

(ii) If $f'(c) = 0$ and $f''(c)$ is positive, then $f(x)$ is minimum for $x = c$.

(iii) $f''(c) = 0$ but $f'''(c) \neq 0$, then $x = c$ is a point of inflexion.

(iv) $f(x)$ is maximum if $f'(x + h)$ changes sign from (+) to (–).

(v) $f(x)$ is minimum if $f'(x + h)$ changes sign from (–) to (+) as h, being numerically infinitely small changes from (–) to (+).

---

(10)

INTEGRAL CALCULUS

1. Fundamental Properties :

(i) Integration is reverse process of differentiation,

i.e., $\int \frac{d\{f(x)\}}{dx}\,dx = f(x) + c$

(ii) $\int cf(x)\,dx = c\int f(x)\,dx$

(iii) $\int \{f_1(x) \pm f_2(x) \pm f_3(x) \pm ...\}\,dx$

$= \int f_1(x) \pm \int f_2(x) \pm ...$

2. Fundamental Results :

(i) $\int x^n\,dx = \frac{x^{n+1}}{n+1} + c$, when $n \neq -1$.

(ii) $\int \frac{dx}{x^n} = -\frac{1}{(n-1)x^{n-1}} + c$, when $n \neq 1$.

(iii) $\int dx = x + c$

(iv) $\int \frac{dx}{\sqrt{x}} = 2\sqrt{x} + c$

(v) $\int \frac{dx}{x} = \log_e |x| + c$

(vi) $\int e^{mx}\, dx = \frac{e^{mx}}{m} + c$

(vii) $\int e^x\, dx = e^x + c$

(viii) $\int a^x\, dx = \frac{a^x}{\log_e a} + c\,(a > 0)$

(ix) $\int \sin mx\, dx = -\frac{\cos mx}{m} + c$

(x) $\int \sin x\, dx = -\cos x + c$

(xi) $\int \cos mx\, dx = \frac{\sin mx}{m} + c$

(xii) $\int \cos x\, dx = \sin x + c$

(xiii) $\int \sec^2 x dx = \tan x + c$

(xiv) $\int \text{cosec}^2 x dx = - \cot x + c$

(xv) $\int \sec x . \tan x dx = \sec x + c$

(xvi) $\int \text{cosec}\, x . \cot x dx = - \text{cosec}\, x + c$

(xvii) $\int \sin h\, x dx = \cos h\, x + c$

3. Standard Results :

(i) $\int \frac{f'(x)}{f(x)} dx = \log_e |f(x)| + c$

(ii) $\int \tan x\, dx = \log_e |\sec x| + c$

(iii) $\int \cot x \, dx = \log_e |\sin x| + c =$

$-\log_e |\operatorname{cosec} x| + c$

(iv) $\int \operatorname{cosec} x \, dx = \log_e \left|\tan \frac{x}{2}\right| + c$

$= \log_e |\operatorname{cosec} x - \cot x| + c$

(v) $\int \sec x \, dx = \log_e \left|\tan\left(\frac{\pi}{4} + \frac{x}{2}\right)\right| + c$

$= \log_e |\sec x + \tan x| + c$

(vi) $\int \frac{dx}{x^2 + a^2} = \frac{1}{a} \tan^{-1} \frac{x}{a} + c$,

when $a \neq 0$.

(vii) $\int \frac{dx}{x^2 - a^2} = \frac{1}{2a} \log_e \left|\frac{x - a}{x + a}\right| + c$,

when $|x| > |a|$.

(viii) $\int \frac{dx}{a^2 - x^2} = \frac{1}{2a} \log_e \left|\frac{a + x}{a - x}\right| + c$,

when $|x| < |a|$.

(ix) $\int \frac{dx}{\sqrt{x^2 \pm a^2}} =$

$$\log_e \left| x + \sqrt{x^2 \pm a^2} \right| + c$$

(x) $\int \frac{dx}{\sqrt{a^2 - x^2}} = \sin^{-1} \frac{x}{a} + c$

(xi) $\int \frac{dx}{x\sqrt{x^2 - a^2}} = \frac{1}{a} \sec^{-1} \frac{x}{a} + c$

(xii) $\int \frac{dx}{x\sqrt{x^2 - 1}} = \sec^{-1} x + c$

(xiii) $\int \sqrt{x^2 \pm a^2}\, dx$

$$= \frac{x\sqrt{x^2 \pm a^2}}{2} \pm \frac{a^2}{2} \log_e$$

$$\left| \left(x + \sqrt{x^2 \pm a^2} \right) \right| + c$$

(*xiv*) $\int \sqrt{a^2 - x^2}\, dx$

$$= \frac{x\sqrt{a^2 - x^2}}{2} + \frac{a^2}{2}\sin^{-1}\frac{x}{a} + c$$

(*xv*) $\int f(ax+b)dx = \frac{F(ax+b)}{a} + c$

(*xvi*) $\int e^x \{f(x) + f'(x)\}\, dx = e^x f(x) + c$

(*xvii*) $\int e^{ax} \cos bx\, dx$

$$= \frac{e^{ax}(a\cos bx + b\sin bx)}{a^2 + b^2} + c$$

(*xviii*) $\int e^{ax} \sin bx\, dx$

$$= \frac{e^{ax}(a\sin bx - b\cos bx)}{a^2 + b^2} + c$$

4. Methods of integration :

(*a*) Transformation Methods :

(*i*) Simple algebraic processes

(*ii*) Rationalisation

(*iii*) Partial fraction

(*iv*) Trigonometrical transformations

(*b*) Integration by parts :

(*i*) $\int u.v\,dx$

$$= u\int v dx - \int\left\{\left(\int v dx\right).\left(\frac{du}{dx}\right)\right\} dx$$

(*ii*) Choose first function in the order : Inverse Trigonometrical function, Logarithmic, Algebraic, Trigonometrical, Exponential function.

(*c*) Integration by substitution: change one variable by another suitable one, so that function is easily integratable.

5. Definite Integrals :

Rule : $\int_a^b f(x)\,dx = \mathrm{F}(b) - \mathrm{F}(a)$

(*i*) $\int_a^a f(x)\,dx = 0$

(*ii*) $\int_a^b f(x)\,dx = \int_a^b f(y)\,dy$

(*iii*) $\int_a^b f(x)\,dx = -\int_b^a f(x)\,dx$

(iv) $\int_a^b f(x)dx = \int_a^c f(x)dx + \int_c^b f(x)dx$, [if $a < c < b$].

(v) $\int_0^a f(x)\,dx = \int_0^a f(a-x)\,dx$

(vi) $\int_0^{na} f(x)\,dx = n\int_0^a f(x)\,dx$, if $f(a+x) = f(x)$

(vii) $\int_0^{2a} f(x)\,dx = 2\int_0^a f(x)\,dx$, if $f(2a-x) = f(x)$

$= 0$, if $(2a - x) = -f(x)$

(viii) $\int_{-a}^{+a} f(x)\,dx = 2\int_0^a f(x)\,dx$, if $f(-x) = f(x)$

$= 0$, if $f(-x) = -f(x)$

(ix) $\int_0^{\pi} \sin x\,dx = 2\int_0^{\pi/2} \sin x\,dx$

(x) $\int_0^{\pi} \cos x\,dx = 0$

(xi) $\int_0^{\infty} \frac{\sin bx}{x}\,dx = \frac{\pi}{2}$ or $\frac{-\pi}{2}$ as $b >$ or < 0

(xii) $\int_0^{\infty} \frac{\sin x}{x}\,dx = \frac{\pi}{2}$

(*xiii*) $\int_0^{\pi/2} \log \sin x \, dx$

$$= \int_0^{\pi/2} \log \cos x \, dx = \frac{\pi}{2} \log \frac{1}{2}$$

6. Area of plane curves :

(*a*) **Cartesian co-ordinates :**

(*i*) If the curve be $y = f(x)$,

$$\text{Area} = \int y dx$$

(*ii*) If two curves be $y = f(x)$, $z = g(x)$;

$$\text{Area} = \int |f(x) - g(x)| \, dx$$

(*b*) **Polar co-ordinate :** If the curve be

$r = f(\theta)$: Area $= \frac{1}{2} \int r^2 \, d\theta$

(*c*) **Important areas :**

(*i*) Area of the ellipse : $\frac{x^2}{a^2} + \frac{y^2}{b^2} = 1$ is πab.

(*ii*) Area of the circle : $x^2 + y^2 = a^2$ is πa^2.

7. Important Tricks about substitution :

(i) $(a^2 - x^2)$ and its power,
put $x = a \sin \theta$

(ii) $(a^2 + x^2)$ and its power,
put $x = a \tan \theta$

(iii) $(x^2 - a^2)$ and its power,
put $x = a \sec \theta$

(iv) $(a - x)$ and its power,
put $x = a \sin^2 \theta$

(v) $(a + x)$ and its power,
put $x = a \tan^2 \theta$

(vi) $(x - a)$ and its power,
put $x = a \sec^2 \theta$

(vii) $\sqrt{\dfrac{a-x}{a+x}}$, put $x = a \cos \theta$ or write it as

$\dfrac{a-x}{\sqrt{a^2 - x^2}}$ and then put $x = a \sin \theta$

(viii) Like $\cos \sqrt{x}$, $\sin (\log \tan^{-1} x)$, $\sec^2 (x e^x)$;

put $\sqrt{x} = y$, $x e^x = y$, $\log \tan^{-1} x = y$ etc.

(ix) $\int_0^{\pi/2} \sin^n x dx$

$$= \int_0^{\pi/2} \cos^n x dx$$

$$= \frac{n-1}{n}, \frac{n-3}{n-2}, \frac{n-5}{n-4}, \ldots$$

$$\frac{3}{4}, \frac{1}{2}, \frac{\pi}{2} \text{ (for } n \text{ even)}$$

$$= \frac{n-1}{n}, \frac{n-3}{n-2}, \frac{n-5}{n-4}, \ldots \frac{4}{5}, \frac{2}{3}$$

(for n odd)

11

SET THEORY

1. Algebraic laws and basic set operations.

(i) Primary laws:

(a) $A \cap A = A$

(b) $A \cup A = A$

(c) $A \cup \phi = A$

(d) $A \cap \phi = \phi$

(ii) Commutative laws :

(a) $A \cup B = B \cup A$

(b) $A \cap B = B \cap A$

(iii) Associative laws :

(a) $A \cup (B \cup C)$
$= (A \cup B) \cup C$

(b) $A \cap (B \cap C)$
$= (A \cap B) \cap C$

(iv) Distributive laws :

(a) $A \cup (B \cap C)$
$= (A \cup B) \cap (A \cup C)$

(b) $A \cap (B \cup C)$
$= (A \cap B) \cup (A \cap C)$

(v) D'Morgan's laws :

(a) $(A \cup B)' = A' \cap B'$

(b) $(A \cap B)' = A' \cup B'$

(c) $A - (B \cup C)$
$= (A - B) \cap (A - C)$

(d) $A - (B \cap C)$
$= (A - B) \cup (A - C)$.

2. If n stands for number of elements of a set then,

(i) $n(A \cup B) = n(A) + n(B) - n(A \cap B)$

(ii) For disjoint sets $n(A \cup B) = n(A) + n(B)$

(iii) For the two sets A & B, the number of elements of only A (having unique property) $= n(A) - n(A \cap B)$

(iv) For three sets $n(A \cup B \cup C) = n(A) + n(B) + n(C) - n(A \cap B) - n(B \cap C) - n(A \cap C) + n(A \cap B \cap C)$.

(v) For three sets, the number of elements of only A (having unique property) $= n(A) - n(A \cap B) - n(B \cap C) - n(A \cap C) + n(A \cap B \cap C)$

3. An ordered pair is of form (a, b). a is known as first co-ordinate and b as second co-ordinate.

If $a \neq b$, then $(a, b) \neq (b, a)$.

4. Let A and B be two non-empty sets then,
   (a) $A \times B = \{(x, y)/x \in A, y \in B\}$
   (b) $n(A \times B) = n(A) \times n(B)$
   (c) $A \times (B \cap C) = (A \times B) \cap (A \times C)$
   (d) $A \times (B \cup C) = (A \times B) \cup (A \times C)$
   (e) $(A - B) \times C = (A \times C) - (B \times C)$

5. **Formulae for Relations :**
   (a) A relation R on a set A is a subset of $A \times A$.
   (b) A relation R from set A to set B is subset of $A \times B$.
   (c) Reflexive relation : A relation R is reflexive when $x\text{R}y \vee x \in A$.
   (d) Transitive relation : A relation R is transitive when $x\text{R}y \wedge y\text{R}z \Rightarrow x\text{R}z$.
   (e) Symmetric relation : A relation R is symmetric when $x\text{R}y \Rightarrow y\text{R}x$.
   (f) A relation which is reflexive, symmetric and transitive is said to be an equivalence relation.

6. **Mapping :** Let there be two non-empty sets A and B. Then if there is a rule or a correspondence f, which associates each element of A with one and only one element of B, then f is said to be a mapping from A to B and we write as $f : A \rightarrow B$.

where, A is known as domain of f and B co-domain of f

Thus, if A = {1, 2, 3, 4} and B = {1, 4, 8, 13} then, $f(x) = x^2$ is a mapping from A to B.

But, if A = {1, 2, 3, 4} and B = {1, 4, 8}, then $f(x) = x^2$ is not a mapping from A to B, as element $3 \in A$ has no image on set B.

12

STATISTICS

1. Mid-point or, Mid value or class mark,

$$x = \frac{\text{lower limit} + \text{upper limit}}{2}$$

2. Range = Maximum value of a variate – minimum value of the variate.

3. Mean $(M_x) = A + C\frac{\Sigma d_i f_i}{N}$

where, A = Assumed mean

C = Length of the class.

d_i = Deviation

$$= \frac{x_i - \text{Assumed mean}}{C}$$

f_i = Frequency and N = Total number of frequencies

4. Median $= 1 + \dfrac{\frac{N}{2} - c_f}{f} c$;

where : l = lower limit of the middle class, c_f = cumulative frequency of the pre-middle class and f = frequency of the middle class.

5. Mode $= l + \dfrac{f_m - f_0}{2f_m - f_0 - f_1} \times c$

Model class : The class having maximum frequency.

where : l = lower limit of the model class,
f_1 = frequency of the past class,
f_m = frequency of the model class and
f_0 = frequency of the pre-model class.

6. Standard deviation,

$$\sigma_x = c \times \sqrt{\frac{\Sigma d_i 2 f_i}{N} - \left(\frac{\Sigma f_i d_i}{N}\right)^2}$$

7. Variance $= \sigma^2{}_x = \dfrac{\Sigma f_i x_i^2}{N} - \left(\dfrac{\Sigma f_i x_i}{N}\right)^2$

8. Mean deviation :

$$\text{M.D.} = \frac{\sum_{i=1}^{n} |x_i - \text{M}| f_i}{\text{N}}$$

where : M = Mean or median or mode.

(*a*) when a new variate $u_i = \dfrac{x_i - a}{c}$ is introduced, then

(*i*) $\overline{u} = \dfrac{\Sigma f_i u_i}{\text{N}}$, and $\overline{x} = a + c.\overline{u}$.

(*ii*) $\sigma u_i^2 = -\dfrac{\Sigma f_i \sigma_x^{\ 2}}{\text{N}} - \left(\dfrac{\Sigma f_i u_i}{\text{N}}\right)^2$, and

$$\sigma_x^{\ 2} = c^2 \sigma u_i^2 .$$

13

PROBABILITY

1. Probability of even E :

$$P(E) = \frac{n(E)}{n(S)}$$

2. $0 \le P(E) \le 1$
3. $P(E') = 1 - P(E)$
4. $P(E_1 - E_2) = P(E_1) + P(E_2) - P(E_1 \cap E_2)$
5. When E_1 and E_2 are mutually exclusive then, $P(E_1 \cup E_2) = P(E_1) + P(E_2)$.
   Here, $P(E_1 \cap E_2) = 0$
6. $$P(E_1 \cap E_2) = P(E_1) \times P\left(\frac{E_2}{E_1}\right)$$

   $$= P(E_2) \times P\left(\frac{E_1}{E_2}\right)$$
7. When E_1 and E_2 are independent:
   $P(E_1 \cap E_2) = P(E_1) \times P(E_2)$

In this case $P\left(\frac{E_2}{E_1}\right) = P(E_2),\ P\left(\frac{E_1}{E_2}\right) = P(E_1)$

and $P\left(\frac{E_2}{E_1}\right) = \frac{P(E_1 \cap E_2)}{P(E_1)}$

8. Union (sum) means **or**. Intersection (product) means **and.**
9. E_1 and E_2 are complementary events if they are mutually exclusive and happening of any one of them is a must.
10. $P(A \cap B) \leq P(A) : P(A \cap B) \leq P(B);$
    $P(A \cap B \cap C) \leq P(A \cap B), P(B \cap C), P(C \cap A)$
11. $P(A \cup B) \geq P(A); P(A \cup B) \geq P(B)$
    $P(A \cup B \cup C) \geq P(A \cup B), P(A \cup C), P(B \cup C)$
12. $P\{(A \cup B)'\} = \{1 - P(A)\}\{1 - P(B)\}.$
13. $P(A \cup B) = 1 - P(A').\ P(B').$
    where A and B are independent events.
14. *(a)* Odds in favour of E $= \frac{P(E)}{P(E')}$

    (b) Odds against of E $= \frac{P(E')}{P(E)}$

    (c) $P(E) + P(E') = 1$

15. Baye's theorem : If A be an event which can occur only with one of the mutually exclusive events $B_1, B_2, B_3 \ldots B_n$ then,

$$P\left(\frac{B_i}{A}\right) = \frac{P(B_i)\, P\left(\frac{A}{B_i}\right)}{\sum_{i=1}^{n} P(B_i)\, P\left(\frac{A}{B_i}\right)}.$$

16. The probability of getting exactly r successes in n independent trials of an experiment is given by:

${}^nC_r P^r q^{n-r}$ where, $r = 0, 1, 2, \ldots n$; P is the probability of success and q that of failure in a single trial.

17. $P(s) = 1$ and $P(\phi) = 0$; where : s and ϕ are certain and impossible events respectively.

---

(14)

DETERMINANTS

1. General form of a determinant of third order:

$$\Delta = \begin{vmatrix} a_1 & b_1 & c_1 \\ a_2 & b_2 & c_2 \\ a_3 & b_3 & c_3 \end{vmatrix}$$

2. The minor of a constituent is defined as the determinant which is obtained after removing the row and column through that constituent:

i.e., minor of $b_3 = \begin{vmatrix} a_1 & c_1 \\ a_2 & c_2 \end{vmatrix}$

3. The co-factor of any element in a determinant is its minor with the proper sign. The sign of an element in the ith row and j^{th} column is $(-1)^{i+j}$. The co-factor of an element is usually denoted by the corresponding capital letter.

Thus, the co-factor of $b_3 = (-1)^{3+2} \times$ minor of b_3;

$$i.e., B_3 = -\begin{vmatrix} a_1 & c_1 \\ a_2 & c_2 \end{vmatrix}$$

4. **Laplace's expansion:** A determinant can be expanded in terms of any row (or column) as follow:

$$\Delta = a_1A_1 + b_1B_1 + c_1C_1$$

$$= a_1\begin{vmatrix} b_2 & c_2 \\ b_3 & c_3 \end{vmatrix} - b_1\begin{vmatrix} a_2 & c_2 \\ a_3 & c_3 \end{vmatrix} + c_1\begin{vmatrix} a_2 & b_2 \\ a_3 & b_3 \end{vmatrix}$$

$$= a_1(b_2c_3 - b_3c_2) - b_1(a_2c_3 - a_3c_2) + c_1(a_2b_3 - a_3b_2)$$

Also, $\Delta = b_1B_1 + b_2B_2 + b_3B_3 = a_3A_3 + b_3B_3 + c_3C_3$.

5. **Properties of determinants:**

   (a) If rows are changed into columns and columns into rows, the value of the determinant does not change

$$i.e., \begin{vmatrix} a_1 & b_1 & c_1 \\ a_2 & b_2 & c_2 \\ a_3 & b_3 & c_3 \end{vmatrix} = \begin{vmatrix} a_1 & a_2 & a_3 \\ b_1 & b_2 & b_3 \\ c_1 & c_2 & c_3 \end{vmatrix}$$

(b) If two rows (or two columns) are interchanged, the value of the determinant changes in sign, but the magnitude does not change:

i.e., $\begin{vmatrix} a_1 & b_1 & c_1 \\ a_2 & b_2 & c_2 \\ a_3 & b_3 & c_3 \end{vmatrix}$

$= -\begin{vmatrix} c_1 & b_1 & a_1 \\ c_2 & b_2 & a_2 \\ c_3 & b_3 & a_3 \end{vmatrix}$

$= +\begin{vmatrix} c_1 & a_1 & b_1 \\ c_2 & a_2 & b_2 \\ c_3 & a_3 & b_3 \end{vmatrix}$

(c) If in a determinant, two rows (or two columns) are same (identical), the value of the determinant = 0.

i.e., $\begin{vmatrix} a_1 & a_1 & b_1 \\ a_2 & a_2 & b_2 \\ a_3 & a_3 & b_3 \end{vmatrix} = 0.$

(d) Multiplying every element in a row or column by a constant k, has the effect of multiplying the determinant by k:

$$i.e., \begin{vmatrix} a_1 & b_1 & kc_1 \\ a_2 & b_2 & kc_2 \\ a_3 & b_3 & kc_3 \end{vmatrix}$$

$$= k \times \begin{vmatrix} a_1 & b_1 & c_1 \\ a_2 & b_2 & c_2 \\ a_3 & b_3 & c_3 \end{vmatrix}$$

(e) If the elements of any row or column be the sum of two or more quantities, the determinant can be expressed as the sum of two or more determinants of the same order.

$$i.e., \begin{vmatrix} a_1 & b_1 + k_1 & c_1 \\ a_2 & b_2 - k_2 & c_2 \\ a_3 & b_3 - k_3 & c_3 \end{vmatrix}$$

$$= \begin{vmatrix} a_1 & b_1 & c_1 \\ a_2 & b_2 & c_2 \\ a_3 & b_3 & c_3 \end{vmatrix} + \begin{vmatrix} a_1 & k_1 & c_1 \\ a_2 & -k_2 & c_2 \\ a_3 & -k_3 & c_3 \end{vmatrix}$$

(*f*) The value of a determinant does not change if a multiple of a row (or column) is subtracted from or added to any other row (or column)

i.e.,
$$\begin{vmatrix} a_1 & b_1 & c_1 \\ a_2 & b_2 & c_2 \\ a_3 & b_3 & c_3 \end{vmatrix}$$

$$= \begin{vmatrix} a_1 & b_1 - ka_1 & c_1 + ma_1 \\ a_2 & b_2 - ka_2 & c_2 + ma_2 \\ a_3 & b_3 - ka_3 & c_3 + ma_3 \end{vmatrix}$$

(15)

DYNAMICS

1. Laws of Motion under gravity :

(a) Momentum $= mv$

(b) Force, $P = mf$

$$= m\frac{d^2s}{dt^2} = m\frac{dv}{dt} = mv\frac{dv}{ds}$$

(c) $R = m(g + f)$ and $R = m(g - f)$ are reactions of mass m moving upward and downward respectively on a horizontal plane, like as lift.

2. Uniform velocity :

(a) Resolved parts of velocity V of a particle moving at (x, y) after time t along co-ordinate axes OX and OY are

$$\frac{dx}{dt} = v\cos\alpha, \quad \frac{dy}{dt} = v\sin\alpha.$$

(b) Parallelogram of velocities : For the resultant W of two velocities u and v,

$$\frac{dx}{dt} = u + v\cos\alpha, \quad \frac{dy}{dt} = v\sin\alpha.$$

$$W = \sqrt{\left(\frac{dx}{dt}\right)^2 + \left(\frac{dy}{dt}\right)^2}$$

$$= \sqrt{u^2 + v^2 + 2uv\cos\alpha}$$

For direction,

$$\frac{dy}{dx} = \tan\theta = \frac{v\sin\alpha}{u + v\cos\alpha}$$

(c) If u be the velocity of a river, y be its breadth and v be the velocity of swimmer, then the time taken by him to cross the river through shortest path,

$$t = \frac{y}{\sqrt{v^2 - u^2}}, \text{ when } v > u$$

$$\text{or } t = \frac{y}{\sqrt{u^2 - v^2}}, \text{ when } u > v.$$

For minimum time path $= \dfrac{y}{v}$.

3. Acceleration:

(a) If a particle is moving at $P(x, y)$ after

time t, then $\frac{dx}{dt}, \frac{dy}{dt}$ and $\frac{d^2x}{dt^2}, \frac{d^2y}{dt^2}$ are components of its velocity v and acceleration f along X and Y axis respectively.

$$v = \sqrt{\left(\frac{dx}{dt}\right)^2 + \left(\frac{dy}{dt}\right)^2}$$

$$f = \sqrt{\left(\frac{d^2x}{dt^2}\right)^2 + \left(\frac{d^2y}{dt^2}\right)^2}$$

(b) Basic formulae : $v = \frac{ds}{dt}$,

$$f = \frac{dv}{dt} = v\frac{dv}{ds} = \left(\frac{d^2y}{dt^2}\right).$$

$$v = u + ft,$$

$$s = ut + \frac{1}{2}ft^2 ; v^2 = u^2 + 2fs.$$

(c) Distance described during n^{th} second

$$= \int_{t=n-1}^{n} (u + ft)dt = u + \frac{1}{2}(2n-1)f.$$

(*d*) Average velocity $= \frac{1}{2}(u+v)$

$$= u + \frac{1}{2}ft.$$

(*e*) Retardation $= -f$.

4. Vertical Motion under Gravity :

(*a*) For upward motion : g is negative

(*i*) $\frac{dy}{dt} = u - gt$

(*ii*) Greatest height $= \frac{u^2}{2g}$

(*iii*) Total time of flight $= \frac{2u}{g}$

(*iv*) $g = 32$ ft/sec^2 or 981 cm/sec^2

(*v*) Time to ascend = Time to descend

$$= \frac{u}{g}$$

(*b*) For downward motion : g is positive

(*i*) $v = \sqrt{2gh}$

(*ii*) $t = \sqrt{\frac{2h}{g}}$, when falling freely from a height h.

(c) For upward motion on an inclined plane:

(i) $$\frac{ds}{dt} = u - gt \sin \alpha$$

(ii) Total time $= \dfrac{2u}{g \sin \alpha}$

(d) Time to slide down any chord of a vertical circle $= \sqrt{\dfrac{2d}{g}}$;
where d = diameter of the circle.

5. Projectile motion :

(a) For the projectile moving at (x, y) after t seconds,

$$\frac{dx}{dt} = u \cos \alpha, \quad \frac{dv}{dt} = u \sin \alpha - gt.$$

(b) Equation of the path of the projectile

$$y = x \tan \alpha - \frac{g \sec^2 \alpha}{2u^2} x^2$$ or

$$y = x\left(1 - \frac{x}{R}\right) \tan \alpha$$

(c) (i) Range (R) $= \dfrac{u^2 \sin 2\alpha}{g}$

(ii) Time of flight $= \dfrac{2u \sin \alpha}{g}$

(iii) Greatest height (H) $= \dfrac{u^2 \sin^2 \alpha}{2g}$.

(d) Maximum range $= \dfrac{u^2}{g}$, when $\alpha = 45°$

(e) For a given u the same range is possible

for $\alpha = \dfrac{\theta}{2}$ or $\left(90° - \dfrac{\theta}{2}\right)$; where : θ is an

angle for which the value of $\dfrac{Rg}{u^2}$ is a

proper fraction.

(f) Maximum range on a plane inclined at

$$\beta_0 = \frac{u^2}{g(1 + \sin \beta)}$$
